# Cross-Cultural Analysis of Image-Based Assessments:

## Emerging Research and Opportunities

Lisa Keller
*University of Massachusetts Amherst, USA*

Robert Keller
*Measured Progress, USA*

Michael Nering
*Measured Progress, USA*

A volume in the Advances in
Knowledge Acquisition, Transfer,
and Management (AKATM) Book
Series

Published in the United States of America by
IGI Global
Information Science Reference (an imprint of IGI Global)
701 E. Chocolate Avenue
Hershey PA, USA 17033
Tel: 717-533-8845
Fax: 717-533-8661
E-mail: cust@igi-global.com
Web site: http://www.igi-global.com

Library of Congress Cataloging-in-Publication Data

Names: Keller, Lisa, 1971- author. | Keller, Robert, 1968- author. | Nering,
    Michael L., author.
Title: Cross-cultural analysis of image-based assessments : emerging research
    and opportunities / by Lisa Keller, Robert Keller, and Michael Nering.
Description: Hershey, PA : Information Science Reference, [2018] | Includes
    bibliographical references.
Identifiers: LCCN 2017008843| ISBN 9781522526919 (h/c) | ISBN 9781522526926
    (eISBN)
Subjects: LCSH: Visual perception--Testing. | Visual perception--Research.
Classification: LCC BF241.4 .K45 2018 | DDC 152.14--dc23 LC record available at https://lccn.
loc.gov/2017008843

This book is published in the IGI Global book series Advances in Knowledge Acquisition, Transfer, and Management (AKATM) (ISSN: 2326-7607; eISSN: 2326-7615)

British Cataloguing in Publication Data
A Cataloguing in Publication record for this book is available from the British Library.

All work contributed to this book is new, previously-unpublished material.
The views expressed in this book are those of the authors, but not necessarily of the publisher.

For electronic access to this publication, please contact: eresources@igi-global.com.

# Advances in Knowledge Acquisition, Transfer, and Management (AKATM) Book Series

ISSN:2326-7607
EISSN:2326-7615

Editor-in-Chief: Murray E. Jennex, San Diego State University, USA

### MISSION

Organizations and businesses continue to utilize knowledge management practices in order to streamline processes and procedures. The emergence of web technologies has provided new methods of information usage and knowledge sharing.

The **Advances in Knowledge Acquisition, Transfer, and Management (AKATM) Book Series** brings together research on emerging technologies and their effect on information systems as well as the knowledge society. **AKATM** will provide researchers, students, practitioners, and industry leaders with research highlights surrounding the knowledge management discipline, including technology support issues and knowledge representation.

### COVERAGE

- Cognitive Theories
- Cultural Impacts
- Information and Communication Systems
- Knowledge acquisition and transfer processes
- Knowledge management strategy
- Knowledge Sharing
- Organizational Learning
- Organizational Memory
- Small and Medium Enterprises
- Virtual Communities

IGI Global is currently accepting manuscripts for publication within this series. To submit a proposal for a volume in this series, please contact our Acquisition Editors at Acquisitions@igi-global.com or visit: http://www.igi-global.com/publish/.

# Titles in this Series

*For a list of additional titles in this series, please visit:*
*http://www.igi-global.com/book-series/advances-knowledge-acquisition-transfer-management/37159*

**Bio-Inspired Computing for Information Retrieval Aplications**
D.P. Acharjya (School of Computing Science and Engineering, VIT University, India) and
Anirban Mitra (Vignan Institute of Technology and Management, India)
Information Science Reference ● ©2017 ● 388pp ● H/C (ISBN: 9781522523758) ● US $205.00

**Managing Knowledge Resources and Records in Modern Organizations**
Priti Jain (University of Botswana, Botswana) and Nathan Mnjama (University of Botswana,
Botswana)
Business Science Reference ● ©2017 ● 280pp ● H/C (ISBN: 9781522519652) ● US $185.00

**Analyzing the Role of Citizen Science in Modern Research**
Luigi Ceccaroni (1000001 Labs, Spain) and Jaume Piera (ICM-CSIC, Spain)
Information Science Reference ● ©2017 ● 355pp ● H/C (ISBN: 9781522509622) ● US $185.00

**Scholarly Communication and the Publish or Perish Pressures of Academia**
Achala Munigal (Osmania University, India)
Information Science Reference ● ©2017 ● 375pp ● H/C (ISBN: 9781522516972) ● US $190.00

**Open Source Solutions for Knowledge Management and Technological Ecosystems**
Francisco J. Garcia-Peñalvo (University of Salamanca, Spain) and Alicia García-Holgado
(University of Salamanca, Spain)
Business Science Reference ● ©2017 ● 297pp ● H/C (ISBN: 9781522509059) ● US $195.00

**Handbook of Research on Social, Cultural, and Educational Considerations of Indigenous
Knowledge in Developing Countries**
Patrick Ngulube (University of South Africa, South Africa)
Information Science Reference ● ©2017 ● 462pp ● H/C (ISBN: 9781522508380) ● US $265.00

**Research 2.0 and the Impact of Digital Technologies on Scholarly Inquiry**
Antonella Esposito (University of Milan, Italy)
Information Science Reference ● ©2017 ● 343pp ● H/C (ISBN: 9781522508304) ● US $185.00

*For an enitre list of titles in this series, please visit:*
*http://www.igi-global.com/book-series/advances-knowledge-acquisition-transfer-management/37159*

701 East Chocolate Avenue, Hershey, PA 17033, USA
Tel: 717-533-8845 x100 ● Fax: 717-533-8661
E-Mail: cust@igi-global.com ● www.igi-global.com

# Table of Contents

# Preface

Social media platforms are inundated with quizzes to predict almost everything about ourselves, such as our philosophy of life, what we should do with our lives, the perfect career, our soulmate, etc. However, most of these "quizzes" are clearly not serious, and do not seem to be valid in anyway; they are more for fun and entertainment. However, the idea of using images to learn more about people in a scientific way is gaining popularity. These types of assessments are fun, engaging and the results are interesting, even when you know that the instrument is not necessarily valid. With the ubiquity of technology, and the ability to read larger, more diverse audiences relatively easily and cheaply, the promise of visual assessments is high. These types of tools require little to no language, making them more easily adaptable to different languages and cultures. Images are easy to process, and provide more information quickly than text-based questions. Given these promises, the need to apply scientific rigor to these assessments is crucial so that they can be used with greater confidence.

One area of particular interest for us was the ability to use these assessments across different cultures without having to translate large amounts of text. The issue of translating assessments is large, and requires not just a strict translation of text into another language, but an adaptation of the meaning of that text to different cultures. This is a time-consuming and expensive task. Images, however, require no translating, so might be perfect for use in cross-cultural assessments. We must be careful, however, to be sure that the images are interpreted the same way across cultures, and do our due diligence in ascertaining that this is true. This book provides an introduction to visual assessments, and provides an example of the development and evaluation of a particular visual assessment. Although the research in this area is still in its infancy, the results of this research have shown great promise in our ability to identify images that transcend culture.

This book is written with limited technical detail, and is intended to serve as a conceptual introduction to the development of visual assessments. While there is some statistical work done in the book, for readers without a lot of statistical background, the book should still be enjoyable. The book was written for those interested in development of image-based assessments with a scientific process, and key ideas to consider when developing a tool that might be used across multiple cultural contexts. We hope you find this book enjoyable and useful.

# Introduction

Our society is being bombarded with visual information through technology. Youtube, social media, and the Internet are supplying content in an increasing amount in visual form. Instead of text, videos are provided for disseminating information on a large number of topics. Our communication is turning more visual through the use of Facetime, and communication applications like Snapchat; this phenomenon is especially true for the younger generation, who has had technology their entire lives. This barrage of visual information requires a renewed attention to visual literacy, so that we can understand the information that is coming at us from all angles. Understanding how to interpret and evaluate visual information is not a new skill, but its importance is magnified as the amount of visual information in our daily lives increases. To be savvy and critical consumers of this information, attention needs to be given to this skill in the same way that is has historically been given to evaluating the credibility of text-based information.

Visual information has advantages over text-based information in that it is easier to process, and can communicate large amounts of information more efficiently. Furthermore, it is more engaging to the consumer of the information, so it sustains attention. Given that as a culture visual information has become such a norm, there is a need to capitalize on the ability of technology to transmit visual information in even more parts of life. While visual information has laid claim to many aspects of life, when it comes to assessments, text is still the predominant format. There have been some changes in that with the ubiquity of internet quizzes on social media, even though those are typically silly quizzes designed for entertainment purposes, answering questions like "What state are you from?" or "What kind of eggs are you?" Although these quizzes are generally not taken seriously by the test-takers, the designers of the quizzes are using them to collect information from the users of the quizzes. These quizzes have the potential to become more than just entertainment. Since there are a large number of people who enjoy taking these quizzes the natural extension is to use the format of these fun quizzes in a serious way, to use as actual, scientifically based assessments, designed to measure constructs of interest. To date, the largest use of these types of assessments is in psychology, with the predominance in personality measures. Although there are companies using these types of personality measures in serious contexts, the science behind them is not necessarily well documented for the general public.

One promising feature of image-based assessments is that they can be constructed to be text-free. While the newer types of assessments that mirror the Internet quizzes typically do utilize text in conjunction with the images, there is no reason to assume that it is essential. In fact, by eliminating text all together, the assessments become usable by those with low, or limited literacy as well as with those who speak different languages. In traditional text-based assessments a long process of adaptation is required to be able to administer them in other languages to ensure that the assessment means the same thing in another culture. Not only does the text need to be translated, it needs to be adapted so that the spirit of the text, not just the literal translation of the text, is achieved. When there is no text to translate, using the assessment across cultures is simplified. This feature offers the production of assessments with great flexibility and utility.

The purpose of this book is to explore the utility of using image-based assessments across cultures. This exploration begins with a justification for the need for such assessments (Chapter 1), and a discussion of visual literacy, along with research regarding the features of images do and don't translate across cultures (Chapter 2). Then, visual assessments that currently exist are reviewed, and their applicability to different cultures is discussed (Chapter 3). The types of bias that need to be considered in cross-cultural assessments and methods for assessing that bias are presented (Chapter 4). Two studies are then presented where an attempt to create a personality assessment that can be used in two different cultures is presented (Chapter 5), and the book concludes with some directions for future research in this area (Chapter 6). At the end of each chapter, practical take-home tips from the chapter are presented for a practitioner, where applicable.

# Chapter 1
# Overview and Benefits of Visual Assessments

## ABSTRACT

*This chapter presents a motivation for why it is essential that assessments move toward incorporating images, whether in conjunction with text, or instead of text. A discussion of the motivation stemming from a technologically savvy and media saturated generation with limited attention span general creates a need to update the thinking around assessments. This discussion is followed by an overview of what visual assessments are, and how they have been used historically. The benefits of visual assessments are detailed along with the limitations of visual assessments. A discussion of the power of images over text are presented along with familiar examples of how we use images to communicate information in a clear, concise and quick fashion are presented. The chapter concludes with examples of some visual assessments in use, although greater detail is reserved for Chapter 2.*

## WHY VISUAL ASSESSMENTS?

Online quizzes are all over the Internet. Anyone on social media has encountered quizzes named "Where should you live?" or "What kind of dog would you be?" These quizzes are extremely popular, and range from interesting to absurd. BuzzFeed is responsible for many of these popular quizzes, and even the most absurd ones get attention. For example, there is a quiz entitled "Pick A Disney Sidekick And We'll Predict When You'll Get Married." The most

DOI: 10.4018/978-1-5225-2691-9.ch001

popular story of 2013 in the New York Times was an article about the quiz designed to determine where you live based on how you pronounce certain words (Meyer, 2014). While most people likely understand that these quizzes are just for fun, and not scientific, it does not stop them from taking them, and sharing their results with their friends on social media. The BuzzFeed quiz "Which State Do You Actually Belong In" got over 40 million views (Associated Press, 2014).

Why are these quizzes so popular, even if they have no scientific merit? There are many blog posts that explore this question, and one important aspect of these quizzes being popular is the ability to share the results on social media (Associate Press, 2014). Some of the most popular quizzes are personality quizzes, with 70% of the top 100 quizzes being personality quizzes (Haynam, 2014). While personality quizzes are not new, their popularity and people's enthusiasm for them is. According to the New York Post, one of the reasons these personality quizzes are so popular is that "Those questions are easier to answer than a real personality test…It's very easy to say, 'This is the candy that I like, this is the movie that I like.' You can turn it into some information about yourself—without actually doing the hard work of really thinking hard about yourself" (Associate Press, 2014)

When tracking the most popular features of the top 100 quizzes, Haynam (2014) noted that 90% of them used images in the questions, and 100% used images in the results. Further, 75% of the traffic is from social media (Tamkin, 2014). Historically, personality quizzes, even in popular culture venues such as Seventeen Magazine, have been text-based questions rather than image-based questions, and were less interactive, since they were presented in print rather than on computer. The introduction of technology, making the quizzes more visually appealing, easier to answer with less introspection, and social media, allowing the results to be shared immediately, and with everyone, appears to have created a phenomenon that people just can't get enough of.

## A New Generation

In addition to the new presentation of information as quizzes, people are changing along with the technology. There is now a generation of people who have been raised with technology, and are avid consumers of this technology. They are active on social media, and have become accustomed to the flair that it is provided through technology. According to InSites Consulting, Generation Y, or Millennials, belongs to 2.5 social media networks on average, and

80% of this generation logs onto social media daily (van den Bergh, 2014) and 98% are online (Zickuhr & Rainie, 2014). While Millennials do read, and actually read more than previous generations (Tamkin, 2014) they read *differently* than previous generations. One professor, in an attempt to make a textbook more desirable to her Millennial students found that creating a text that was more visual, devoid of any extraneous text, and written in a more engaging manner was well received by her students, where traditional texts were not (Millennial Marketing, n.d.). They tend to scan for information, and only absorb relevant text. The theory is that it is because they were raised with the Internet, and bombarded with an enormous amount of information, which requires the ability to scan to find important information; previous generations did not have to contend with that. In fact, it is hypothesized that the data immersion has provided this generation with "the visual skills that make them superior scanners." In fact, Millennials are "capable of taking in a lot of visual information at once, probably more than older generations, provided it is presented in an attractive and easily digestible way. This makes good design as important, if not more important, than good writing" (Millennial Marketing, n.d.). Given these types of change, to engage these types of readers, and learners, visual presentation of material is at the core, and less is more when it comes to text.

In terms of communicating with others, texting has become more popular than talking. A 2014 Gallup Poll showed that the number of texts was greater than the number of phone calls made, with 68% of Millennials indicating that they text many times during the day (Newport, 2014). Because of some of the limitations of texting, including the inability to express tone effectively in such a compressed communication style, apps like Viber and Line are trying to introduce more visual-based messaging, rather than text-based messaging (Howe, 2015). Among teen users, usage of Facebook and other text-based social media sites declined in 2014, while increases were found in image-based social media sites such as Instagram and Pinterest (Beck, 2014). Snapchat, a picture-based texting app is worth over $19 Billion (Nusca, 2015). According to Statistics Brain Research Institute (http://www.statisticbrain.com), over 34 billion images have been uploaded to Instagram. Further, Instagram reportedly has the most engaged users of any social media platform, where users don't have anything to click on and follow, and so their attention remains on the content at hand (Jackson, 2015). As an example, the following two Instagram posts from McDonald's (Figures 2 and 3) received more attention than all of McDonald's tweets for the entire day (Jackson, 2015). In the image shown in Figure 1, followers were ask to click on their favorite breakfast item.

*Figure 1.*

Then viewers were presented with the image presented in Figure 2.

In fact, the processing of visual information is so important to the new generation of learners, that the Common Core State Standards (National Governors Association Center for Best Practices & Council of Chief State School Officers, 2010) include standards related to visual literacy. It is believed that since we live in such an image-saturated environment, it is impossible to thrive without understanding how to interpret visual images. Visual literacy refers to the ability to interpret, use, and create visual media.

Clearly, this generation, and most likely future generations, responds more readily to image-based information rather than text-based information, in virtually all aspects of life. As such, it is important that we update our tools to respond to the needs of the new generation of learners. This includes updating our assessment practices to include more images, with careful attention on how those images are constructed and interpreted by learners.

*Figure 2.*

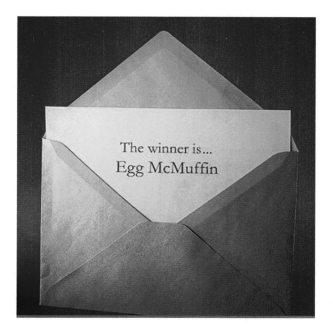

## WHAT IS A VISUAL ASSESSMENT?

Visual assessments, sometimes referred to as pictorial assessments, or image-based assessments, are assessments that rely on pictures, or images, rather than text, as a way of measuring a variety of constructs. Therefore, instead of reading a test question, a picture or image is presented, and the person taking the assessment is asked to react to that image in some way. While not assessments, the example of traffic signs may illustrate the utility of such assessments. Many traffic signs are presented visually instead of, or in addition to, using text. This is a purposeful choice; the shape of the stop sign, yield sign, and merge sign are quite distinctive in providing information to the driver without requiring the driver to read any text.

While most drivers can probably read, the visual information can serve multiple purposes. First, the driver does not need to be able to read the language in which the text is written. For safety concerns it is essential that we all recognize the stop sign, regardless of whether that sign is written in a language that we can read.

Secondly, the visual information is processed more readily in the brain (Cowen, 1984). So, while you might be able to read the word STOP on the

*Figure 3.*

*Figure 4.*

sign, you don't need to since you immediately recognize the symbol of the stop sign, and can react more quickly. Again, for safety reasons, being able to react quickly is a benefit.

## Benefits of Visual Assessments

First and foremost, the changing times, changing population of people, and the growth of technology essentially mandate the need for a change in assessment if we want to keep the current generation engaged. While there might be some that complain that the new generation is not able to concentrate, and should be trained to tolerate the more traditional assessments, the truth is that assessments need to change with the times, just as other industries have changed with the times. Despite these complaints, there are many benefits to using visual assessments beyond appealing to a generation of people who are accustomed to consuming more visual information. There are benefits inherent to this type of assessment that should be realized regardless of the change in the media culture.

While the safety concern does not exist in assessments as in traffic situations, there are similar benefits to using images over text in certain circumstances. Similar to that of the traffic sign, the benefit to the visual assessment is the amount of information that can be transmitted in an efficient manner. We have all heard the expression that a picture is worth a thousand words. That is not just a cliché, but also has some basis in scientific fact. The processing of images is different than the processing of text, whereby images are processed more holistically than verbal presentations of the same material (Domzal & Unger, 1985). Our brain is actually wired to process visual information not only more quickly, but also better than other types of information (Ware, 2004). Pictures are categorized more quickly than words (Snodgrass & Vanderward, 1980), and images are especially useful if the goal is to produce an emotional response (Rossiter & Percy, 1980).

As early as 1979, Salomon (1979) found that people learn abstract information more easily when presented both visually and verbally, and Cowen (1984) posited that visual media makes information more accessible to a given person than text media. In 2009, Willingham posed the simple question asking why students appear to remember everything they see on television but very little that they hear in a lecture (Willingham, 2009). This is due to the fact that visual media can aid in the retention of ideas.

Why is processing visual information so much easier than processing text? One theory (Parkinson, 2011) is that it is because we react to the images both cognitively and emotionally. From the cognitive standpoint, visual cues help to process information more readily, attracting attention to specific aspects of the information that is being communicated. Because images usually elicit an emotional reaction as well, this stimulates other areas of the brain, which helps us to understand information more fully. Additionally, since images are processed in our long-term memory, while text is processed in our short-term memory, they are easier to remember than text. Taken together, using images in addition to, or instead of, text can create a more powerful means to transmit information than using text alone.

A secondary benefit comes from the issue of language. Translating assessments into different languages, or more accurately, adapting assessments for different languages and cultures, is an intensive task, both in terms of the cognitive aspect, and as a result, the financial aspect. The more languages that you might want to translate that test into, the more resource investment required. Using a text-free, or image-based assessment would eliminate the need for translation, so long as the reaction to the images is not culture specific. The task of translation or adaptation can be reduced to testing for the cultural equivalence of the images, rather than the translation of test items into many languages. Images that are free from cultural differences can be selected, and the assessment is automatically available to all people within those cultures.

The field of intercultural communication has recognized many of the benefits of using images to aid in comprehension of material across cultures. Not only do the images themselves relieve the burden of needing text, but also combining text and visuals together offers "double cues for understanding," and also supports seeing the big picture instead of becoming mired in details (Bresciani, 2013). Bresciani (2013) also notes that while the benefits of using visuals in cross-cultural contexts are many, there are still open questions as to whether the principles of vision are universal across cultures, and to the extent that differences exist, these advantages might not be fully realized. However, these are *open* questions, meaning that there is not the literature to support, or not support, the universality of vision or interpretation of images, and it is essential to continue to investigate the universal natures of visual communication, especially given the importance in cross-cultural contexts.

# Limitations of Visual Assessments

While visual assessments offer much promise and clear benefits, they are not without their own limitations. Individual interpretation of the images is likely more variable than individual interpretation of text. There may be aspects of the images that draw the attention of individuals that were not intended to draw focus, creating some ambiguity in the information that the image is intended to elicit. Different people might respond differently to images that include depictions of people, where they like or enjoy pictures or images that contain people that look like themselves over other pictures, simply due to the fact that the people in the picture look similar to themselves (Furl, 2016), which may not be the purpose of using this image to assess a psychological construct. This becomes especially problematic when using the visual assessments across different cultures.

While visual assessments have the advantage of serving many more populations of examinees more easily than text-based assessments, there are groups of examinees that will have greater difficulty with image-based assessments than text-based assessments. For instance, examinees that are visually impaired, color-blind, or have visual processing issues will have difficulty with visual assessments. Providing accommodations in these cases might be more difficult than providing accommodations in more traditional text-based assessments, limiting the utility of these types of assessments with certain populations.

It is worth reiterating that in relation to the cross-cultural promise offered by visual assessments, the greatest limitation lies in the how accessible the same images are across cultures. While the language issue is avoided, the reactions that images evoke might also vary across cultures. There is so little research in this area that it is difficult to know how difficult the challenge to create visual assessments that can transcend culture will be. However, given the potential gains, it is necessary to do the research to determine how to do it well.

Although visual assessments have great promise, given these limitations it is essential that image-based assessments be evaluated with respect to both their validity and generalizability across subgroups. Regardless of whether one is measuring constructs that have been typically measured using text-based assessments, or designing an image-based assessment of constructs that have not previously been measured, it essential to demonstrate that the assessment is measuring what we think it is measuring. Since these types of assessments have not been widely used, their psychometric properties have not been widely established. Adapting methodologies used on text-based assessments is a reasonable first step in understanding the power of using visual assessments.

## Historical Uses of Visual Assessments

Although assessments that rely on images are not new, the type of visual assessments that have been used is certainly different than what is ubiquitous in the social media realm. The assessments might not be as visually engaging, relying on older technology and the need to print large numbers hard copies of assessments, which typically meant not using color or complex imagery. Further their use has been in very specific and specialized contexts. Primarily, pictorial assessments have been used for young children, who are pre-literate, or for students with disabilities that might have a difficult time with text-based assessments. Other applications include using visual assessments with populations of people that have limited proficiency in the language. All of these applications exist because the users of the materials were unable to access the text; that is, the image-based assessment was an accommodation, while the text-based format would be considered a preferred option. This is in contrast to the current work being done where image-based assessments are viewed as the preferred mode of assessment. The difference between these contexts is that the image-based assessment is not viewed as being an adaptation, intended to measure the same information as a text-based assessment, it is intended to be the only version of the assessment.

Businesses have recognized the appeal of using images over text for decades and have used this advantage in marketing strategies. An oft-cited statistic is that the human brain processes images 60,000 times faster than it processes text, and 93% percent of human communication is visual (Pant, 2015). These statistics are often attributed to work at the company 3M, but the research is not readily available to the public. Whether or not this statistic is true, research has shown that the brain can identify images that have been seen for only 13 milliseconds (Potter, Wyble, Hagmann, & McCourt, 2014), indicating that images are processed very quickly in the brain. Further, 40 percent of nerve fibers connected to the brain connect to the retina (Golden, 2015). Marketers have used this information to change their strategies, especially as the human attention span reduces (Berger, Remington, Leitner, & Leviton, 2015); there just isn't time to rely on consumers to read text.

While the context in assessment is different than marketing, as people become more accustomed to image-based information, their patience and attention span for text becomes compromised, making the traditional text-based assessments more difficult for people to attend to. By creating visual assessments, the examinees can process information more quickly, as they are engaging in this activity in their lives daily through social media, the Internet, television and video games.

As technology has touched most aspects of life, for most people, the infusion of technology into assessments is natural, and necessary. While computers are used more routinely in assessments, the changes to the assessments themselves have been more about the mode of delivery, rather than on the type of assessment. That is, multiple-choice assessments are still staples in many arenas, but now they are delivered on the computer, rather than on paper and pencil. This "advance" can make testing more efficient, and scoring easier; however, it does not fully harness the power of technology. Thus, not only is using an image-based assessment potentially easier, it is in line with other activities of life, making these assessment, perhaps, more natural, more engaging, and less burdensome to examinees.

Educators have capitalized on the ease of processing visual information and have incorporated this idea into teaching and learning; however, the idea of using images in assessments has not made much progress. This may be due to several reasons, the least of which is the ease and expense of producing visual assessments as opposed to text based assessments. Text-based assessments are easier and cheaper to produce, especially if the images require color printing. In present times, with the ubiquity and availability of technology, these concerns are reduced, and producing assessments based on images are not only practical and possible, but may offer advantages over text based assessments, especially in the light of globalization, and online learning. As more and more University classes move to online platforms, either in whole or part, the need to visually represent information, and then to assess students, is only increasing.

## Examples of Visual Assessments

While the Internet quizzes are example of visual assessments, most of them are not scientifically based, and are, for the purposes here considered as entertainment quizzes rather than actual assessments. One of the most common uses of visual assessment comes from the health field. The pain scale is a very common tool used to assess the level of pain in patients, when responding might be difficult. Figure 5 provides a common depiction of the level of pain a patient might be experiencing.

Other visual assessments have been used in health care as well to provide better access to healthcare in cases where caregivers may have lower levels of education or a lack of literacy. Lower literacy makes using diagnostic instruments such as health questionnaires or other assessment tools difficult or impossible (Leiner, Peinado, Villanos, & Jimenez, 2013). These differences in access to communication or assessments may make it difficult for physicians to accurately diagnose issues, provide appropriate follow-up care, or even provide accurate communication to caregivers. In these contexts, visual assessments have been included to improve health outcomes in at-risk populations. For example, an assessment to improve the obesity risk of low-income students includes images for parents to respond to (Townsend, Shilts, Styne, Allen, Drake, & Ontail, 2015). Figure 6 demonstrates an image from that assessment.

Pictorial information has also been used in consent forms for treatment (Fuller, Dudley, & Blacktop, 2002). Since providing consent means that the patient understands the information being provided, it is important that the content of the consent be understood. In this example, the issue was not necessarily low verbal skill, but the nature and complexity of the information being shared. In many cases, the information provided to give consent involves probabilities. Since many people have difficulty understanding probability, a pictorial representation, shown in Figure 7, was used to increase understanding, and to ensure that that patient was capable of giving consent.

The use of the pictorial consent did increase the understanding of the content in the patient sample (Fuller, Dudley, & Blacktop, 2002).

*Figure 5.*

| No pain | Discomforting | Distressing | | Intense | | Utterly horrible | Unimaginable unspeakable |

| 0 | 1 | 2 | 3 | 4 | 5 | 6 | 7 | 8 | 9 | 10 |

| | Very mild | | Tolerable | | Very distressing | | Very intense | | Excruciating unbearable | |

*Figure 6.*

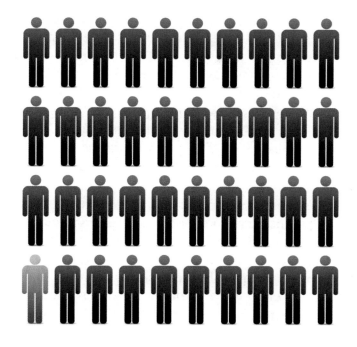

*Figure 7.*

**Question 1**

  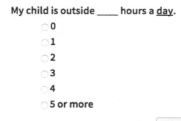

Perhaps the greatest diversity in pictorial assessments has been observed in psychological assessments. Image-based assessments have been used to study interests (vocational and avocational), aggression, personality, psychopathology, and assessing family structures for the purposes of clinical therapy. There are differences between the assessments in the use of images.

The majority of the assessments intend for the respondents to view the image in a similar way; that is the images are created to mean something specific that would, hopefully, be consistent across test takers. In contrast, images could be used in a projective sense, where the images are intentionally vague, and it is how the test taker interprets the image that is of interest. This projective technique might be used to study particular personality traits such as extraversion or narcissism. The majority of the assessments use the images in a straightforward manner, with images designed to reflect specific information for the test taker. The exception is the aggression inventory, which is a projective assessment, where the interpretation of the test taker is the response of interest.

When considering the psychometric quality of the tests, these tests often had reasonable psychometric properties, although the quality of the tests did tend to vary depending on the subgroup of respondents being used in the analysis. These results are not surprising given the variety of test takers that are of interest in using an image-based assessment, and this outcome is not uncommon, even in more traditional, text-based assessments. These assessments, along with their psychometric quality, will be described more fully in Chapter 2.

## SUMMARY

The use of visual assessments certainly is not without any complications, but the benefits of this type of assessment are certainly exciting. Reducing the language demand for the user would allow greater access to the assessments

*Figure 8.*

Take Home Tips

Image-based assessments:
- reduce language requirements for respondents
- are more engaging and fun
- are more consistent with today's visual culture
- might help with cross-cultural assessment

across many groups of people. The power and value of images has been used in many contexts, including safety, education, marketing and transportation. Extending the use of images to assessments is a natural extension of the importance of images in our society.

# REFERENCES

Associated Press. (2014). Why online quizzes are taking over your Facebook feed. *New York Post*. Retrieved from http://nypost.com/2014/02/24/why-online-quizzes-are-taking-over-your-facebook-feed/

Beck, M. (2014, October 8). *This Survey Says: Teens Are Fleeing Facebook; Instagram & Twitter Are More Popular*. Retrieved from http://marketingland.com/survey-says-teens-fleeing-facebook-103174

Berger, I., Remington, A., Leitner, Y., & Leviton, A. (2015). Brain development and the attention spectrum. *Frontiers in Human Neuroscience*, *9*, 23. doi:10.3389/fnhum.2015.00023 PMID:25698956

Bresciani, S. (2013). Organizational communication with visual mapping: Comparing East and West. In D. Ingehoff (Ed.), *Internationale PR-forschung*. Konstanz: UVK Verlag.

Cowen, P. S. (1984). Film and text: Order effects in recall and social inferences. *Educational Communication and Technology*, *32*, 131–144.

Domzal, T. J., & Unger, L. S. (1985). Judgments of verbal versus pictorial presentations of a product with functional and aesthetic features. *Advances in Consumer Research. Association for Consumer Research (U. S.)*, *12*, 268–272.

Fuller, R., Dudley, N., & Blacktop, J. (2002). How informed is consent? Understanding of pictorial and verbal probability information by medical inpatients. *Postgraduate Medical Journal*, *78*(923), 543–544. doi:10.1136/pmj.78.923.543 PMID:12357016

Furl, N. (2016). Facial-attractiveness choices are predicted by divisive normalization. *Psychological Science*, *27*(10), 1379–1387. doi:10.1177/0956797616661523 PMID:27565534

Golden, F. (2015, February 11). *The power of visual content: Images vs text*. Retrieved from https://www.eyeqinsights.com/power-visual-content-images-vs-text/

Haynam, J. (2014, November 4). *What the top 100 most viewed interact quizzes all have in common* [Interact Blog]. Retrieved from https://www.tryinteract.com/blog/what-the-top-100-most-viewed-interact-quizzes-all-have-in-common/

Howe, N. (2015, July 15). *Why Millennials Are Texting More And Talking Less*. Retrieved from http://www.forbes.com/sites/neilhowe/2015/07/15/why-millennials-are-texting-more-and-talking-less/#17fbb3955761

Jackson, D. (2015, October 12). *Twitter vs. Instagram: Which is Best for Your Brand?* Retrieved from http://sproutsocial.com/insights/twitter-vs-instagram/

Leiner, M., Peinado, J., Villanos, M. T. M., & Jimenez, P. (2013). Assessment disparities among pediatric patients: Advantages of pictorial descriptions. *Frontiers in Pediatrics*, *1*, 28. doi:10.3389/fped.2013.00028 PMID:24400274

Meyer, R. (2014, January 17). The New York Times' Most Popular Story of 2013 Was Not an Article. *The Atlantic*. Retrieved from http://www.theatlantic.com/technology/archive/2014/01/-em-the-new-york-times-em-most-popular-story-of-2013-was-not-an-article/283167/

Millennial Marketing. (n.d.). *Do Millennials Read? Yes, But They Read Differently*. Retrieved from http://www.millennialmarketing.com/2010/05/do-millennials-read-yes-but-they-read-differently/

National Governors Association Center for Best Practices & Council of Chief State School Officers. (2010). *Common Core State Standards*. Washington, DC: Authors.

Newport, F. (2014, November 10). *The new era of communication among Americans*. Retrieved from http://www.gallup.com/poll/179288/new-era-communication-americans.aspx

Nusca, A. (2015, February 19). *Why Snapchat is worth $19 billion (or more)*. Retrieved from http://fortune.com/2015/02/19/snapchat-worth-19-billion-more/

Pant, R. (2015, January 16). *Visual marketing: A picture's worth 60,000 words*. Retrieved from http://www.business2community.com/digital-marketing/visual-marketing-pictures-worth-60000-words-01126256#BJEeyFZQfsKszvkg.99

Parkinson, M. (2011, December 5). *We process visuals 60,000 times faster than text – Here's why.* Retrieved from https://rhdeepexploration.wordpress.com/2011/12/05/visuals-60000-times-faster/

Potter, M. C., Wyble, B., Hagmann, C. E., & McCourt, E. S. (2014). Detecting meaning in RSVP at 13 ms per picture. *Attention, Perception & Psychophysics, 76*(2), 270–279. doi:10.3758/s13414-013-0605-z PMID:24374558

Rossiter, J. R., & Percy, L. (1980). Attitude Change Through Visual Imagery in Advertising. *Journal of Advertising, 9*(2), 10–16. doi:10.1080/00913367.1980.10673313

Snodgrass, J. G., & Vanderwart, M. (1980). A standardized set of 260 pictures: Norms for name agreement, image agreement, familiarity, and visual complexity. *Journal of Experimental Psychology. Human Learning and Memory, 6*(3), 174–215. doi:10.1037/0278-7393.6.2.174 PMID:7373248

Tamkin, E. (2014, September 11). *Millennials are Better-Read, Vastly Superior to Rest of Population, Says Science.* Academic Press.

Townsend, M., Shilts, M., Styne, D., Allen, L., Drake, C. & Ontail, L. (2015). Healthy kids obesity risk assessment demonstrates predictive validity in sample of low-income children. *The FASEB Journal, 29*(1).

van den Bergh. (2014, October 14). *Millennials & social media: The what, where and why.* Retrieved from http://www.insites-consulting.com/infographic-millennials-social-media/

Zickuhr, K., & Rainie, L. (2014, September 10). *Younger Americans and Public Libraries.* Retrieved from http://www.pewinternet.org/2014/09/10/younger-americans-and-public-libraries/

# Chapter 2
# Visual Literacy and Global Understanding

## ABSTRACT

*Visual literacy is taking on new importance in the media saturated culture in which we all live. Everyone is inundated with visual stimulation each day and with the amount of time spent on the computer, and with social media, that stimulation is not likely to decline. The result is a need to be able to critically evaluate visual information in the same way that we have been taught to critically read written text. This is the field of visual literacy, and while it has existed for some time, it has become the focal point of many twenty-first century skills frameworks. It is no longer optional to be able to understand visual information. This chapter explains what visual literacy means, and how cultural differences impact the interpretation of visual information.*

## WHAT IS VISUAL LITERACY?

Generally speaking, visual literacy refers to the ability that enables an individual to interpret and create images. Visual literacy is not a new idea or concept, and has existed from as early as the 1960s. However, the role and place of visual literacy has changed dramatically with the introduction of the Internet. Historically, visual literacy was discussed in the context of visual arts, and was really supplemental to other types of literacy. Our society has become so visual with technology that visual literacy is no longer a luxury, but is essential for all people in society. With the emergence of the central

DOI: 10.4018/978-1-5225-2691-9.ch002

focus of visual literacy, there have been a host of types of literacies defined relative to the consumption of media, and the definitions vary and are in flux, and are under the larger umbrella of "21$^{st}$ Century Skills" or "21$^{st}$ Century Literacy." (Jones & Flannigan, 2006) The components of these literacies are:

- Digital Literacy
- New Media Literacy
- Information Literacy
- Lateral Literacy: Hypermedia and Thinking
- Photo-visual Literacy
- Reproduction Literacy
- Today's Literacy
- Visual Literacy

Definitions for all of these literacies are not provided here, as not all of them are relevant to issues involved in developing visual assessments, specifically visual assessments that are culturally flexible; that is, they can be used across multiple cultures. This list is provided to illustrate the complexity of literacy in the technology age, where people are interacting with media in new and increasingly complex ways. The most relevant type of literacy for the purposes of this book is Visual Literacy. While there are myriad definitions of Visual Literacy, the themes of the definitions are very similar. The Association of College and Research Libraries (ACRL) defines Visual Literacy in a Higher Education environment as the ability to:

- Determine the nature and extent of the visual materials needed
- Find and access needed images and visual media effectively and efficiently
- Interpret and analyze the meanings of images and visual media
- Evaluate images and their sources
- Use images and visual media effectively
- Design and create meaningful images and visual media
- Understand many of the ethical, legal, social, and economic issues surrounding the creation and use of images and visual media, and access and use visual materials ethically.

The most salient aspect of visual literacy in terms of engaging with a visual assessment is "interpret and analyze the meanings of images and visual media." The ACRL identifies four performance indicators associated with this standard. These are:

1.  The visually literate student identifies information relevant to an image's meaning.
2.  The visually literate student situates an image in its cultural, social, and historical contexts.
3.  The visually literate student identifies the physical, technical, and design components of an image.
4.  The visually literate student validates interpretation and analysis of images through discourse with others.

Taking a closer look at the second indicator, "…situates an image in its cultural, social, and historical contexts" is central to the concern of creating culturally flexible visual assessments. While it is ideal that all adults will be visually literate, assuming that each person situates all images into the proper context, including cultural, is perhaps optimistic. In an academic setting that might be appropriate, however, when interacting with media in non-academic ways, it is unlikely that anyone's reactions and interpretations of images are perfectly situated in the ideal context. However, the importance of this indicator is that it reveals the importance of the context: social, historical, and cultural when interpreting the meaning of images. The implication is that images are not necessarily culturally neutral, but rather that culture will have an impact on the interpretation of the image. As a result, care must be taken when constructing a visual assessment, and images should be chosen that could potentially transcend culture. While it might not be possible to find such images, there is little empirical evidence to suggest whether or not it is possible. There is a limited body of research that indicates that there are cultural differences in interpretations of images, however, that does not mean it is impossible to find images that are culturally neutral, only that care must be taken to do so. A call to action has been expressed in 2007 by Salo-Lee that "Visual literacy also becomes an intercultural challenge. How to make visual information accessible and interesting to different groups of people at both home and abroad?" This call to action is an indication that there is a belief that it is possible to communicate through images to people of multiple cultures, and that not only is it possible, it is our duty as part of visual literacy. The focus of this section is to review the evidence regarding the possibility of finding culturally neutral images, and the factors that should be considered in selecting or developing images that could transcend culture.

# RESEARCH RELATED TO CULTURAL DIFFERENCES IN INTERPRETING IMAGES

One of the key attractive features of developing visual assessments is the relative ease in using the same assessments across multiple cultures without the need for laborious translations or adaptations of the instruments into other languages and cultural contexts. However, there is little evidence surrounding the ability to create images that are culturally neutral. While visual communication is often thought of as a universal way to communicate (think of traffic signs!), there are relatively few research studies that have investigated the use of visual communication across cultures, and most of the research is dated, and may or may not be relevant. Given that the world has effectively shrunk with the ubiquity of technology, most anyone can view images from different cultures and see and imagine what life is like in other places other than where one lives. Video games now allow children (and adults) to play with other players in other countries. Social media has allowed friendships to form among people with similar interests across multiple countries and cultures. As such, the exposure of the general public to other cultures is growing. Keeping this in mind research regarding the role of culture in interpreting images might be limited if it predates the World Wide Web, or social media.

The predominant area of research in the cross-cultural comparisons of visual communication have come from the field of advertising, which has been conducting research in this area for almost forty years. Research indicates that images in advertising are most effective when they are tailored to the specific culture (Albers-Miller, 1996; Usunier & Lee, 2005). For example, a McDonald's advertisement in Western cultures depict an individual eating a meal in the restaurant, while in Asian countries the advertisement shows families and groups of friends eating together in the restaurant, to differentiate the individualistic societies and collectivist societies (Hall, 1976).

Research in anthropology, psychology and philosophy has also shown that culture has an impact on how we understand images. The specifics of these studies are provided in the following section regarding the features of images that appear to be culturally sensitive. For each feature discussed, the research associated with that feature is provided. Although the research is limited, it does indicate that cultural differences exist in how images are interpreted. However, it also provides guidance on how images can be constructed or selected to minimize the cultural effects of the interpretations.

# Cultural-Specific Features of Images

Given the existence of the Worldwide Web generally, and social media in particular, interaction between people of different cultures happens at all times of the day. It is not uncommon for people of any age to interact with people of different cultures around a variety of topics. With the "global village" that the world has become, and the prevalence of images in the transmission of information, the need to determine that these images mean the same things across different cultures is essential. However, given its importance, there is relatively little research regarding how images are interpreted across cultures (Bresciani, 2015). Some of the research has indicated that images do not transcend culture due to the differences in perceptions of visual information. While it is likely true that not all images transcend culture, there likely are images that *do* transcend cultures. When considering whether an image is likely culturally neutral, there are elements of images that have been shown in the literature (e.g., Besciani, 2015) to differ across cultures that should be considered. The elements that are most relevant to the construction of visual assessments are discussed below, and for each element, some implications of these factors for constructing a visual assessment are offered.

## Color

Colors are powerful in terms of transmitting information to the viewer. In Western and European cultures white signifies purity, and this fact is used quite often in films. However, in Eastern cultures, white signifies death and mourning, rather than purity. In Western/European cultures, black is used to signify death/mourning. Similarly, red has been shown to indicate love and danger in Western/European cultures, while it signifies joy or luck in Eastern cultures. Further, preferences for color have been shown to vary across cultures (Choungurian, 1968; Taylor, Clifford, & Franklin, 2012).

Color not only has been shown to have different meanings or preferences in different cultures, but even the identification, or naming of colors varies across cultures. Taylor, Clifford and Franklin (2012) showed that certain African tribes used the same word for blue and black, and had several words for the color green. It is accepted among anthropologists that this variation in identifying colors stems from the fact that people actually perceive color differently (Bornstein, 1975). This may be due to differences in environmental factors. Therefore, the use of colors in images might mean different things to different people, depending on culture, and environment.

## Implications for Visual Assessment

While color might present some challenges across cultures in some contexts, one solution could be to use only grey scale images; this solution, however, might be limiting and might take away from the engagement factor of the image-based assessment. Instead, being mindful of what the colors might represent to the cultures of interest is important. Consider building a personality assessment: when trying to select or create images that elicit personality traits, emotional responses might come into play. Consider the example of measuring optimism/pessimism. An image that shows a person in white might evoke feelings of mourning or pessimism in an Eastern culture, while in a Western culture, it might be seen as more light and optimistic. Of course there are other features of the image other than color that will come into play when interpreting the image; however, showing people exhibiting one emotion while dressed in a contradictory color might cause confusion. Imagine someone dressed in black, in dress that might be more typical of mourning rather than elegant evening wear; if this person is also happy, it might be confusing what the image is trying to convey. To avoid this type of cognitive dissonance, the congruence between the expressions of the people in the image and the dress of the people, including the color, might be essential. Instead of avoiding color, it might be wise to choose colors that are less emotionally charged across the cultures of interest.

Aside from the emotional component of color, the idea that different cultures might see colors differently should also be considered. If color is a central, or important, aspect of the image, it is important that the color is seen similarly across cultures. Taking the example of the color blue, where some African tribes have been shown to not differentiate between blue and black, then if blue is used with some intention in the image, that intention would be lost to the Africans that don't see the color as blue.

The solution is not easy, and care should be taken in the choice of colors, and it is essential that there be empirical data collected to support the choice of images for the cultures of interest. One possible approach is to create/select images where the colors are manipulated and gather data (quantitative or qualitative) regarding how the choice of color affects the interpretation of the image. Given that lack of research in area, it is essential that the data be collected and analyzed when images contain color. Collecting such data would also help inform the construction of image-based assessments generally.

## Focus

What a person chooses to focus on in an image might also be culturally defined. Several researchers have found that people of different cultures focus on different aspects of the same image (Chua, Boland, & Nisbett, 2005; Nisbett, 2003; Nisbett & Miyamoto, 2005). The primary difference appears again to be between Western culture and East Asian culture, where people from Western cultures tend to focus on the main central objects, whereas East Asian people focused more on the context of the scene rather than the main object. This discovery was made through asking for recall of the scene (Nisbett & Miyamoto, 2005) and also through the use of eye-tracking software (Chua et al., 2005). In a similar study, Masuda and Nisbett (2006) studied both Asians and Americans with respect to their ability to notice changes in the background of a picture. The Asians were able to more quickly notice the changes in the background as compared to the Americans. Although not related to viewing images, a more recent study demonstrated that the eye-tracking behavior of Arabs and Spaniards varied when scanning text (Marcos, Garcia-Gravilanes, Bataineh, & Pasarin, 2013).

Bresciani (2015) explores the idea of focus in more detail and provides some theory found in the literature around the possible explanation for why different cultures focus on different aspects of an image. Traditionally, the thinking was that the difference was due to collectivism vs. individualism in the culture (Hall, 1976). However, a new theory has emerged posited by Nesbitt (2003). Nisbett (2003) theorized that the observed differences in focus of visual attention and thought patterns could be the byproduct of differences in the patterns of thought which have been shaped by different philosophical traditions. Nisbett named this theory the *Geography of Thought*. The Geography of Thought contrasts the philosophies of Ancient Greece and China. The Greek tradition emphasized individuality and promoted argumentation as a means to advance knowledge. In contrast, Confucius, condemned abstraction and encouraged looking at an issue from all points of view with social harmony was of central concern, and criticism and argumentation were discouraged (Bresciani, 2015). The implication for processing visual information is that Westerners would more likely prefer abstract and linear visualizations, like flowcharts and timelines, and Easterners would prefer visuals that provided a holistic perspective such as concept maps and visual metaphors (Bresciani, 2015). This idea was partially tested and found to be true when European and Asian people were presented a series of images; Europeans preferred the timeline, and Asians preferred the more holistic image (Bresciani, Tan, & Eppler, 2011). In earlier work, Eppler and Ge (2008) showed empirically the differences between European and Chinese students in how they perceived typical business diagrams.

The implication for choosing images to present to people of different cultures is clear: given different cultures, the what the focus of the image is will vary, so when attempting to communicate information, what might appear to be the obvious focus of the image might not be the obvious focus for all.

## Implications for Visual Assessments

Where the observer chooses to focus attention on the image has vast implications for the design of image-based assessments. When an image is chosen or designed, the composition is chosen with a very specific purpose, to elicit a very targeted response. The person choosing/selecting the image has a clear idea what the image is supposed to represent. However, given the research on focus, the culture of the person will likely influence the elements of the image that are focused on. An American choosing or designing the image would pay attention to the main object in the image, and might essentially ignore the context surrounding the primary subject of the image. Clearly, if the person responding to the image is from an Eastern culture, they will not see it the same way, and the context and background becomes much more important. If the person designing/selecting the image ignores the background/context when selecting the image, then the image is less likely to generalize across both Western and Eastern cultures.

As an example, consider an image designed to measure introversion/extraversion. A photo of a person who is alone outside in the woods taking a walk might represent someone who enjoys solitude, which might represent introversion. To the Western eye, the person being alone will stand out in the image, since that is the main object in the photo, and the background would be viewed as scenery. However, an Eastern eye might not interpret the purpose of the image to be about solitude, but about being in nature. It might not matter if there person is alone or in a group. The purpose of the photo would not translate across the two cultures. As such, it is essential that when constructing these types of assessments, feedback be gotten from respondents of all potential cultures regarding the interpretation of the image.

## Symbolic Conventions

Bresciani and Eppler (2010a) contend that the familiarity with certain symbols or images would influence preference for images. Therefore, the types of images that are most commonly used in a culture are likely to be preferred over images that are foreign. Bresciani (2015) posits that Western cultures are most familiar with visualizations such as mind maps and flow charts while in South America concept maps are most familiar. Indian cultures have a long tradition of visual storytelling, whereas Muslim countries tend not to use images, as their tradition is predominantly oral. A recent study demonstrated that familiarity of the symbolic meaning of certain images influences the interpretation of the images, and that interpretation varies across cultures (Qi, 2013). The conclusion of this study was that images used as metaphors or symbols were more problematic than factual pictures, when various cultures are being exposed to the same visual. Given this line of research, clearly different cultures use images and symbols differently, and using images to represent specific messages might be culturally specific. Further, the ore familiar the image, the more comfort the viewer has with the image, and this might have an impact on how the person responds to, and interprets, the image.

## Implications for Visual Assessments

Clearly the more familiar the image is to a person, the more readily he/she will respond to it. Further, the meaning of the image is likely to differ depending on the familiarity of the image. When constructing a visual assessment, then, the choice of imagery will be very important, as different cultures have familiarity with different types of images. Photographs of might be less susceptible to these problems, as indicated by Qi, provided the photographs are depicting scenarios that occur across the multiple cultures of interest.

Suppose an assessment was trying to measure honesty in a person. Images related to honesty across cultures are likely to vary. A specific example is very powerful. The swastika is a symbol that would be likely universally recognized. A Westerner would interpret that symbol to mean something like hate, division, etc. It would definitely have a negative connotation. However, in ancient Hinduism the swastika represents truth, purity and stability. Therefore, depending on the culture of the person viewing the image, the reaction will be strong, and very different from on another. Given the powerful negative connotation in the West, the image is rarely used, while for other cultures it would inspire feelings of peace. In this example, the issue is not with familiarity, as both cultures would be familiar with the symbol, but rather the meaning of the symbol/image is very different across cultures.

A similar example is the use of hand gestures. Using the gesture where the pointer and middle finger are extended into a "V" shape while the other fingers are curled down indicates peace in the United States. However, in other cultures, even other Western cultures, the same symbol is seen as rude and signifies contempt or defiance of authority. Therefore, if the use of symbols, either in images themselves, or within photographs, different emotions might be evoked in the person viewing the image.

## Direction

In Western cultures, the direction of reading is left to right. In other cultures, such as Arabic and Chinese cultures, the direction is reversed, and reading is done right to left. This has implications for how images are viewed, especially if the intent of the image is to portray any linear information, such as through some kind of flow chart or diagram (Besciani & Eppler, 2010b).

## Implications for Visual Assessments

The direction factor may have some implications for visual assessments, depending on how the image is supposed to be interpreted. Being cognizant of how direction might influence the interpretation of an image is crucial to its success in different cultures. If an image relies up directionality, then it might not be the best choice for inclusion in an assessment that is to be used across non-Western cultures.

## Humor

Humor exists in all cultures, but the expression of that humor varies across cultures (Yue, 2010), and thus using humor across different cultures can lead to confusion. Styles of humor can be categorized as self-enhancing, affiliative, self-defeating, and aggressive (Martin, 2007). While both Western and Chinese cultures do not respond well to aggressive humor (Kuiper et al., 2010), North Americans respond positively to self-enhancing humor, while Chinese cultures do not (Kuiper et al., 2004; Chen & Martin, 2005). One very large distinction between Western and Chinese cultures is that Westerners tend to believe that all people are funny (Martin, 2007), whereas Chinese tend to believe that humor resides with comedians, rather than something that is a trait of all people (Yue, 2010). Similarly, the perception of laughing out loud varies between cultures, with Westerners being more comfortable with laughing in public than Chinese, in general (Xu, 2011, p. 70). These ideas condense to the idea that the occasion where humor is viewed as appropriate likely varies as a function of culture. While it may be appropriate for an American politician to use humor, and that humor to be viewed as a positive quality of that politician, it is unlikely to be viewed positively in China. With the increase in internationalization these distinctions might fade in time, but at present these norms still appear to hold (Yue et al., 2016). As a result, how humor is interpreted and viewed is likely dramatically different across cultures and could cause problems when used cross-culturally.

## Implications for Visual Assessments

Given the culture-specific nature of humor, including humor in an assessment to be used in different cultures would be difficult, and very likely to be unsuccessful. Conveying humor through images, without text, might also be a challenge on its own, and would likely not be beneficial for the assessment. It is probably wise to avoid humor in these cases.

## Visual Metaphors

Although there is evidence that symbols vary across cultures, the idea of visual metaphors is slightly different. Can there be metaphors that are universal? There is evidence that visual metaphors of natural scenes might hold across cultures (e.g., mountain scenes, trees, weather), metaphors involving manmade objects do not translate as well (Besciani & Eppler, 2010b). However, even though the very salient metaphor of the iceberg, as in "it's the tip of the iceberg" is strongly culturally-tied to Western cultures, as it is based on Freud's iceberg model of the unconscious mind, and is not readily understood but those in other cultures (Barnard, 2005). Sports metaphors that symbolize teamwork and cooperation are not universal, as most sports are not universally known, and may have different levels of appeal between men and women (Beamer & Varner, 2008). The image of a dog is positive in Western cultures, and the visual metaphor of the St. Bernard as a rescue animal is common; however, in Muslim countries, the dog is seen as negative and a dirty animal (Hogan, 2007). Advertisers have struggled with finding universal, or standardized metaphors that could be used in a global market (Callow & Schiffman, 1999). The findings of the literature seem to suggest that visual metaphors are culturally influenced, and their use should still be limited.

## Implications for Visual Assessments

While it is likely best to avoid visual metaphors for cross-cultural assessments, there are cultures that are less literal than others, and as such, images might still be interpreted as metaphors and not as literal in some cultures, making it difficult to use images across cultures generally. Therefore, keeping images simpler, and as straightforward as possible while paying attention to any imagery that could be interpreted metaphorically is advised. Getting interpretations of imagery from those of other cultures before using the images would be especially important to be sure that meaning is not being ascribed to the image that is not intended.

Bresciani and Eppler (2010b) consolidated these features into a framework for using images across cultures. There are seven features and guidelines provided for each. This framework is reproduced in Table 1.

*Table 1. Guidelines for each factor (Bresciani & Eppler, 2010b)*

| Factor | Guidelines |
| --- | --- |
| Color | Blue is safest<br>Red has the opposite meaning in China and Western countries: if used, its meaning should be made explicit |
| Direction | Conventionally left to right but the contrary in Arabic: order should be reversed when addressing Arabic cultures. |
| Humor | Should be avoided or used with great caution. |
| Sign and Symbols | Need to be localized (for example using the symbol of chopsticks instead of knife and fork in East Asia). |
| Visual Metaphors | Metaphor of war, non well-known sports, and religion should be avoided. Suitable metaphors are for instance: mountain, weather, garden, bridge. |
| Focus | Be aware that objects in a background area of a picture receive equal attention as objects in the foreground by Asians (attributing the same relevance), but are likely ignored by Westerners. |
| Analytic-Holistic nature of thought | Westerners prefer abstract and analytic diagrams, while East Asians prefer visualizations that show relationships and context. |

*Figure 1.*

> **Take Home Tips**
> When constructing visual assessments for cross-cultural use:
>
> - Blue is the most culturally neutral color; avoid red
> - Reduce any unnecessary background imagery
> - Be mindful of any directionality needed for interpretation (right to left vs. left to right)
> - Symbols and Humor don't translate well across many

Clearly, some of these factors are more relevant than others for the purpose of developing visual assessments. For example, humor is less likely to be included in a visual assessment, whereas issues of color, focus, signs and symbols are likely to exist. Visual metaphors might be included, depending upon the nature of the assessment being constructed. This framework provides a means to aid in the development and evaluation of an assessment before testing to see if the assessment is likely to work across cultures.

## SUMMARY

There are many factors to consider when constructing an image-based assessment that can be used cross-culturally. While this area is still relatively new and emerging, there are some guidelines that exist that can help guide the construction or selection of images that are likely to be more culturally neutral than others. Factors to pay specific attention to are color, the use of symbols, the use of visual metaphors, the context of the image, and the direction that the eyes should flow for interpreting the image (left to right vs. right to left). By being mindful of these characteristics, the potential of the images to transcend culture is increased.

## REFERENCES

Albers-Miller, N. D. (1996). Designing cross-cultural advertising research: A closer look at paired comparisons. *International Marketing Review, 13*(5), 59–75. doi:10.1108/02651339610131397

American Library Association. (2000). *Information Literacy Standards for Higher Education*. Association of College and Research Libraries. Retrieved from http://www.ala.org/acrl/standards/informationliteracycompetency

Barnard, G. (1995). *Cross-cultural communication a practical guide.* London, UK: Cassel.

Beamer, L., & Varner, I. (2008). *Intercultural communication in the global marketplace* (4th ed.). Singapore: McGraw-Hill.

Bornstein, M. H. (1975). The influence of visual perception on culture. *American Anthropologist. New Series, 77*, 774–798.

Bresciani, S. (2015). Do you see what I see? The effect of culture on the reception of visual communication. In S. Poutiainen (Ed.), *Theoretical Turbulence in Intercultural Communication Studies* (pp. 81–100). Newcastle Upon Tyne, UK: Cambridge Scholars Publishing.

Bresciani, S., & Eppler, M. J. (2010a, July). Choosing Knowledge Visualizations to Augment Cognition: The Manager's View. *IEEE Proceedings of the 14th International Conference Information Visualization*. London, UK: IEEE.

Bresciani, S., & Eppler, M. J. (2010b). Glocalizaing visual communication in organizations. In B. Bertagni, M. La Rosa, & F. Salvetti (Eds.), *Glocal working* (pp. 233–251). Milan: Franco Angeli.

Bresciani, S., Tan, M., & Eppler, M. J. (2011, August). *Communicating strategy across cultures with visualization: An experimental evaluation.* Paper presented at the annual meeting of the Academy of Management, San Antonio, TX.

Callow, M. A., & Schiffman, L. G. (1999). A Visual Esperanto? The pictorial metaphor in global advertising. *European Advances in Consumer Research, 4*, 17–20.

Chen, G. H., & Martin, R. D. (2005). Coping humor of 354 Chinese university students. *Chinese Mental Health Journal, 19*, 307–309.

Choungourian, A. (1968). Colour preferences and cultural variation. *Perceptual and Motor Skills, 26*(3c), 1203–1206. doi:10.2466/pms.1968.26.3c.1203 PMID:5675688

Chua, H. F., Boland, J. E., & Nisbett, R. E. (2005). Cultural variation in eye movements during scene perception. *Proceedings of the National Academy of Sciences of the United States of America*, *102*, 12629–12633. doi:10.1073/pnas.0506162102 PMID:16116075

Chua, H. F., Boland, J. E., & Nisbett, R. E. (2005). Cultural variation in eye movements during scene perception. *Proceedings of the National Academy of Sciences of the United States of America*, *102*, 12629–12633. doi:10.1073/pnas.0506162102 PMID:16116075

Eppler, M. J., & Ge, J. (2008). Communicating with diagrams: How intuitive and cross-culutral are business graphics? *Euro Asia Journal of Management*, *18*, 3–22.

Hall, E. T. (1976). *Beyond culture*. New York: Doubleday.

Hogan, C. (2007). *Facilitating multicultural groups. A practical guide*. London: Kogan Page.

Jones, B. R., & Flannigan, S. L. (2006, January 1). *Connecting the Digital Dots: Literacy in the 21ˢᵗ Century*. Retrieved from http://er.educause.edu/articles/2006/1/connecting-the-digital-dots-literacy-of-the-21st-century

Kuiper, N. A., Grimshaw, M., Leite, C., & Kirsh, G. (2004). Humor is not always the best medicine: Specific components of sense of humor and psychological well-being. *Humor: International Journal of Humor Research*, *17*(1-2), 135–168. doi:10.1515/humr.2004.002

Kuiper, N. A., Kazarian, S. S., Sine, J., & Bassil, M. (2010). The impact of humor in North American versus Middle East cultures. *Europes Journal of Psychology*, *6*(3), 149–173. doi:10.5964/ejop.v6i3.212

Marcos, M.-C., Garcia-Gavilanes, R., Bataineh, E., & Pasarin, L. (2013, May). Using eye tracking to identify cultural differences in information seeking behavior. Paper presented at the Workshop Many People, Many Eyes, Paris, France.

Martin, R. A. (2007). *The Psychology of Humor: An Integrative Approach*. Burlington, MA: Elsevier Academic Press.

Nisbett, R. E. (2003). *The geography of thought*. New York: Free Press.

Nisbett, R. E., & Miyamoto, Y. (2005). The influence of culture: Holistic versus analytic perception. *Trends in Cognitive Sciences*, 9(10), 467–473. doi:10.1016/j.tics.2005.08.004 PMID:16129648

Qi, H. (2013). Central Aspects in cross-cultural tourism marketing communication-a study based on Finland's travel brochure for the Chinese market. In C.M. Scmidt (Ed.), Optimiert Zielgruppenansprach, Europaische Kulturen in der Wirtschaftskommunication (pp. 119-147). Springer Fachmedian Wiesbaden. doi:10.1007/978-3-531-19492-9_5

Salo-Lee, L. (2007). Towards cultural literacy. In T. Kaivola & M. Melen-Paaso (Eds.), Education for Global Responsibility-Finnish Perspectives. Ministry of Education.

Taylor, C., Clifford, A., & Franklin, A. (2012). Color preferences are not universal. *Journal of Experimental Psychology: Genera, 141.*

Xu, W. (2011). The classical confucian concepts of human emotion and proper humour. In Humour in Chinese Life and Letters. Pok Fu Lam: Hong Kong University Press.

Yue, X., Feng, J., Lu, S., & Hiranandani, N. (2016). To be or not be humorous? Cross cultural perspectives on humor. *Frontiers in Psychology*, 7. doi:10.3389/fpsyg.2016.01495 PMID:27757091

Yue, X. D. (2010). Exploration of Chinese humor: Historical review, empirical findings, and critical reflections. *Humor: International Journal of Humor Research*, 23, 403–420.

Chapter 3
# Review of Existing Psychological Visual Assessments

## ABSTRACT

*Chapter 3 goes into detail describing a selection of the more popular existing psychological visual assessments in use. A description of each assessment is provided, what the use of the assessment is, an example of what a task would entail, and the available psychometric information about the test. This is followed by an evaluation of how culturally sensitive the instrument has shown to be, or might be expected to be. The purpose of this chapter is to review how historically visual assessments have been used to try to assess psychological constructs in a large-scale manner. Three categories of assessments are reviewed: standard assessments that are typically standardized measures, projective assessments, and next generation assessments.*

## PURPOSE

The purpose of this chapter is to review the more popular existing psychological visual assessments. To do so, we break this down into two categories: assessments that have been in long-time professional, or clinical use, and have been subjected to a greater degree of research, and newer types of visual assessments that are web-based, and have less research to substantiate their psychometric quality. Although newer assessments, these assessments

DOI: 10.4018/978-1-5225-2691-9.ch003

represent the type of visual assessments that are on the cutting edge of psychological assessment, and are more engaging and relevant. These types of assessment are similar to the vision of psychological assessments posited in this book, where images are replacing text to create more engaging assessments that appeal to a more technology-focused generation. The assessments are typically enjoyable to take, short, and still of high quality. As a result, more detail is provided for these limited assessments.

Since most visual assessments have been used in the field of psychology, our review of standardized visual assessments focuses on psychological assessments. The assessments reviewed here are in no way exhaustive, but highlight the most popular image-based assessments. For each assessment, the purpose of the instrument is provided, a description of the tasks is provided, and then the psychometric properties are evaluated. There are two major categories of assessments reviewed: standard assessments, and projective assessments. In that standard assessments, items are presented to the test taker, and there is an expected "correct" response. Projective assessments, on the other hand, are typically designed to be ambiguous in the prompts to elicit underlying psychological processes in the test taker. In this sense, the answers are typically more open-ended, and there is no "correct" answer, but there may be responses that align with particular psychological attributes.

# STANDARD ASSESSMENTS

## Raven's Progressive Matrices

The Raven's Progressive Matrices test is a non-verbal measure of ability of clear-thinking skills, efficient problems solving, abstract reasoning, and ability to learn (Domino & Domino, 2006). It is used typically in employment practices to hire professionals and managers. There are two versions of the test: a standard version that is typically used at the entry-level positions, as well as mid-level positions, and an advanced version that is more commonly used for senior management positions and high level positions ((Domino & Domino, 2006). Among the benefits of the assessment are that they are self-administered, and they are easy to score. Since there is no text to read, the assessment is appealing for use with non-verbal examinees, and can be used regardless of the primary language of the examinee.

There is a lot of information available for the interested reader. There are several websites that provide opportunities to take the test for free. Two sites are: https://www.scribd.com/document/269110369/IQ-Test-Raven-s-Advanced-Progressive-Matrices-PDF-Free-Download or https://www.testingmom.com/cpc/practice-for-the-ravens-test/. The test is owned by Pearson, and details about the assessment can be found at their website: http://www.pearsonclinical.com/psychology/products/100000504/ravens-standard-progressive-matrices.html#tab-details.

## Description of the Tasks

The tasks in the Raven's Progressive matrices are familiar to those that have seen IQ tests. Each item consists of a pattern of geometrical figures, and the test-taker has to figure out the next object in the sequence of figures.

*Figure 1.*

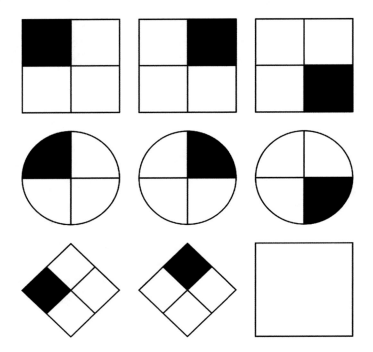

## Psychometric Properties

Both the standard and advanced versions of the test have demonstrated acceptable levels of reliability ($\alpha \geq 0.85$) (Pearson Tech Manual). For validity evidence, convergent validity evidence includes moderate correlations with other measures of cognitive ability, including the American College Test (ACT) and Scholastic Aptitude Test (SAT). The weakness in this evidence is that the Raven's Matrices are not designed to measure what that ACT and SAT are reported to measure, although all three assessments are designed to measure cognitive ability in some way. The technical documentation references individual studies that indicate that the scores on the Raven's Progressive Matrices test correlate with outcomes of interest, including performance in decision-making tasks, ability to attain and retain high-level jobs, ratings of creativity, etc. This evidence is sufficient to indicate that the instrument is psychometrically acceptable, although there is some ambiguity in how the test is designed to measure what it purports to measure.

## Cross-Cultural Use

The Raven's Progressive matrices would appear to be ideal for cross-cultural use, as they do not contain any text, color, or context to influence focus. Indeed, this assessment was originally thought of as "culture-free" or "culture-fair" but is now thought of as "culturally loaded" (Benson, 2003). The reasoning, according to Patricia Greenfield, Ph.D. from the University of California, Los Angeles, is that while the matrix is a common construct in many cultures, it is not common in all cultures. The assessment assumes that the user is familiar with thinking of a matrix as showing rows and columns. When not accustomed to thinking that way, the matrices pose a challenge, and this type of thinking is typically the by-product of traditional schooling, which does not necessarily exist everywhere (Benson, 2003). In a study that included 45 different counturies, cultural differences among the results of Raven's Progressive Matrices were observed (Brouwers, Van de Vijver, & Hemert, 2009). Relative to the framework of Chapter 2, the issue is most likely related to the mode of thinking, "Analytic-Holistic nature of thought" and related to method bias which is discussed in Chapter 4 on measuring cultural equivalence of assessments.

## Pictorial Behavioral Checklist

Due to low levels of literacy in some populations, barriers to receiving proper health care may exist due to communication problems. The Child Behavior Checklist is an instrument that is used to identify behavioral and emotional problems in children. The parent would complete the questionnaire, indicating which behaviors on the checklist their child engages in, and at what frequency. The pictorial version of that instrument, the Pictorial Child Behavior Checklist, was developed to increase comprehension of the checklist for those with lower levels of literacy. There does not appear to be a published version of the instrument, rather researchers have adapted the standard form of the Child Behavior Checklist (Achenbach & Rescorla, 2001) for use in specific settings (Leiner, Rescola, Medina, Blanc, & Ortiz, 2010). The comparability of the standard form and the pictorial form (Leiner, Rescola, Medina, Blanc, & Ortiz, 2010) provides information regarding what the instrument looks like, and reports the success of the adaptation. As such, this instrument, while likely useful, is limited in its use as it is difficult to find a copy of the full instrument, and the researchers would have to be contacted to obtain a version for use.

## Description of the Tasks

The pictorial version of the instrument includes images as well as the text of the questions to aid in comprehension of the questions; it is not a completely image-based assessment. The respondent answer on a 0- to 2-point scale (Not true, Somewhat or Sometimes true, Very often true) to indicate the frequency of the behavior indicated in the item. One item is "Destroys his or her things." The parent, or other responder, indicates how often this behavior occurs. The text is accompanied by an image of a child smashing an object by throwing it, or jumping up and down on top of the object. As such, the respondent would not have to understand the text to understand the behavior being surveyed by the item.

*Figure 2.*

## Psychometric Quality

The psychometric quality of the Pictorial Child Behavior Checklist has been demonstrated to be high. The test-retest reliability of the checklist has been demonstrated to be around 0.92 (Achenbach & Rescorla, 2001), which is quite high.

The psychometric quality of the Pictorial Child Behavior Checklist was compared to the traditional Child Behavior Checklist using low-income Hispanic parents (Leiner, Rescola, Medina, Blanc, & Ortiz, 2010) and found that the psychometric properties of the pictorial version of the checklist were comparable to those of the standard version of the checklist. The two forms were comparable in terms of both validity and reliability. Specifically, reliability was similar, in terms of both test-retest reliability and alternate form reliability. For validity, the two forms performed similarly in terms of being able to discriminate children who visited a community pediatric facility (not related to mental health) from those attending a mental health outpatient clinic. This type of validity evidence is standard in the clinical psychology area.

Given the comparison of the two forms of the checklist, the pictorial version is at least as high quality as the traditional version, with perhaps greater access for parents of lower literacy.

## Cross-Cultural Use

This assessment has been used for different cultures to assess child behavior. However, evaluating the assessment in light of the framework presented in Chapter 2, it would not be surprising if there were cultural bias in this instrument. The instrument is black and white, and the images are line drawings, which limits any cultural issues associated with color. However, the behaviors exhibited in the scenarios on the assessment might not be universally interpreted across cultures. What constitutes problematic behavior in one culture might not constitute a behavioral problem in another culture. Further, the interpretation of what the behavior is that is being illustrated might vary across cultures, and the focus of the attention on the image might be different for different cultures. These issues might make this instrument susceptible to difficulties across cultures.

Most of the research regarding the use of the instrument across cultures has been limited to using the instrument in different cultures to compare the rates of incidence of certain behaviors across cultures, not to examine the use of the instrument across cultures. One study (Jastrowski, Davies, Klein-Tasman, & Adesso, 2009) was found to look at the measurement equivalence of the scale in use with African American youths, which is not necessarily a different culture, but might be indicative of differences for different subgroups. This instrument did not generalize well to this subgroup, and measurement invariance was not supported.

## Picture Anxiety Test

The Picture Anxiety Test is used to assess anxiety and avoidance behaviors in children between the ages of 4 and 8 through a series of vignettes. This instrument is used in conjunction with reports of parents, as the assessment of anxiety in children should be done through multiple reporting sources. The development and content of the assessment is illustrated in the article by Dubi and Schneider (2009). The instrument was demonstrated to work well with children and provides important information, since many measures of children are reports from parents. Since parents might also suffer from anxiety, they might over-report anxious behaviors in their children (Dubi & Schneider, 2009).

## Description of the Instrument

The 17 items on the test are scenarios where a child might demonstrate fearful behavior, such as an encounter with a dog, or a group of children. Two scenarios are presented to the child, one in which the child exhibits fearful behavior, and one in which he/she does not. The gender of the child in the pictures is matched to the gender of the respondent. The child selects the image that they feel exhibits their reaction to the situation.

## Psychometric Quality

Dubi and Schneider (2009) did a comprehensive study of the psychometric quality of the Picture Anxiety Test. The reliability and validity of the instrument was evaluated. Reliability, both internal consistency, and test-retest reliability, was acceptable (over 0.70) and similar to other measures of anxiety. There was evidence of convergent and divergent validity, as indicated by moderate correlations with other measures of anxiety, and low correlations with other

*Figure 3.*

Boy worrying

mental health measures, not specifically related to anxiety. Further, changes in scores on the test were noted after implementing cognitive behavioral therapy with children demonstrating symptoms of anxiety.

The analyses demonstrated high levels of psychometric quality, similar to more traditional measures of anxiety that are text based.

## Cross-Cultural Use

No published research regarding the cross-cultural use of the instrument was found. Evaluating the images relative to the framework presented in Chapter 2, there are some issues that might arise with the cross-cultural use of the assessment, although they might be mitigated by the fact that the assessment is administered individually to children. The images are color line drawings, and not photos; this choice might make representations of different culture difficult with respect to skin tone, features, hair and eye color. However, because they aren't real people, that might have less of an effect on the results of the assessment. The bigger issue might be in the choice of images. For example, in Figure 3 the image is of a boy worrying. The choice of images that depict worrisome topics might not generalize across cultures, and might cause some confusion. However, it is unlikely to be a big problem since the test is individually administered, not self-administered. If there were attempts to make the assessment self-administered via computer, for example, then more thought about the images might be warranted.

## The Dominic-R Pictorial Interview and Dominic Interactive

The Dominic-R pictorial interview is an individually administered interview protocol designed to diagnose mental health issues in young children. An interviewer reads text to the child, the content of which is also illustrated in images. The child responds to the prompt to describe his/her feelings. As an example the following images and prompts might be used:

*Figure 4.*

DO THUNDERSTORMS MAKE YOU FEEL SCARED,LIKE DOMINIC?

This assessment does not require the test-taker to read any text, although the text is provided, if the test-taker desires to read the text, as well as listen to the text being presented by the interviewer. This is especially important in cases where the child might not have the vocabulary to understand what the question is asking (Yates, 1990). The response from the test-taker is a verbal response, and does not require the child to produce text.

The Dominic Interactive is a computer-based version of the Dominic-R instrument, where the child navigates through a series of scenarios that are taken from the Dominic-R instrument. However, this instrument is administered on the computer, and allows for customization of the ethnicity and gender of the child that appears in the scenes. The instrument has been translated into 11 languages. There are prompts that go with each picture, like "Do you often feel useless or guilty?" to which the child responds "yes" or "no." This text is read aloud to the child, so that the child does not have to read the text. The picture illustrates a scenario that is meant to depict the prompt. Unlike the Dominic-R, the Dominic Interactive is colorful and engaging. The assessment takes 15 minutes and is automatically scored by the computer, creating efficiency for the user. This instrument can be found online at http://www.dominic-interactive.com/index_en.jsp.

There were several limitations stated by the distributors of the Dominic Interactive. Some of these limitations would apply to all assessments of children's mental health, while others were more specific to the Dominic Interactive. According to the Dominic Interactive Website (http://www.dominic-interactive.com/24_en.jsp), the following limitations were noted.

General: Social desirability might influence the child's responses, children might lack insight necessary to adequately answer the questions, experiences that happen close to when the instrument is administer might influence the responses due to the fact that children tend to live more in the present. Some more specific limitations that were noted were: The Dominic Interactive provides information regarding tendencies, not specific diagnoses, and the tool is not designed for use for children under the age of 6, or those with developmental delays. These limitations should be taken into account when using and interpreting the results of the Dominic Interactive.

## Psychometric Quality

Fairly intensive analyses of the Dominic-R have been undertaken (Valla, Bergeron, & Smolla, 2000), and the instrument appears to be of adequate psychometric quality. The Dominic-R demonstrated good reliability, with coefficient alpha values of 0.89 on both subscales measured. Validity evidence, while limited, suggests that there is utility in using the Dominic-R for diagnosing mental health issues in children. The Terry Questionnaire was analyzed on a smaller sample to investigate the reliability of this version and while the reliability was slightly lower on the Terry Questionnaire than the Dominic-R (0.79-0.90), it still met acceptable reliability (Valla, Bergeron, & Smolla, 2000).

There have been several studies investigating the psychometric quality of the Dominic Interactive with different samples of children (e.g., Linares Scott et al., 2006; Shojaei et al., 2009). Reliability in all studies has been found to be adequate to high, ranging from 0.70 to .90, depending on the study. Validity was assessed in multiple ways, with good validity evidence provided. The results from the assessment agreed with the diagnoses from expert judgment, significant differences in scores were observed between clinical and non-clinical samples, indicating an ability to discriminate among those with problems and those without problems, and the measure seems to correlate with other measures, although details were not provided regarding the strength of these correlations. Based on the evidence available, the instrument appears to be psychometrically sound.

## Cross-Cultural Use

To be sensitive to differences in ethnicity, the Terry Questionnaire was developed as a version of the Dominic-R that uses an African-American child in the pictures, as opposed to a white child. The Terry Questionnaire has been translated into Spanish, German and French versions.

The interactive version of the assessment, the Interactive Dominic Questionnaire, was developed to be self-administered computer. In this version, the child is presented with the images, and a voiceover describes the situation and asks how the child would react. The child clicks a box indicating YES or NO to various responses. The Interactive Dominic Questionnaire features children that are boy/girl or Latino/white/African-American/Asian.

These variants of the assessment are a good attempt to generalize across different cultures, even if the cultures are all Western cultures. The fact that there was a need to create these variants provides insight into the fact that it should be adapted to be more culturally sensitive. That said, given that the images are black and white line drawings, rather than color drawings or photos, the impact might be lessened. It is difficult to know, as there was no published research regarding the cross-cultural use of the instrument. In addition to the representation of the children, the contexts that might, for example, produce fear, as in Figure 4 might not be generalizable across cultures, either, so the contexts of the images should be reviewed to be sure that they are universally understood if the instrument is to be used across cultures.

## Pictorial Instrument for Children and Adolescents

The Pictorial Instrument for Children and Adolescents was designed to assess psychiatric conditions in children ages 6-16 (Ernst et al., 2004). The assessment is a semi-structured interview and consists of 137 pictures organized into categories according the pathology being assessed. The assessment takes between 40 and 60 minutes to administer. One attractive feature of the instrument is that it can be obtained free of cost from the developer, by contacting her at by mail at Dr. Ernst, NIDA, Brain Imaging Center, 5500 Nathan Shock Drive, Baltimore, MD 21224 or sent by e-mail to mernst@ intra.nida.nih.gov. However, only clinicians with psychiatric training should administer the instrument.

## Description of Tasks

The tasks are simple images representing children in various psychological states. The interviewer prompts the test-taker with prompts such as "Do you feel sad the way he does?" The child can then respond to the question. Interviewers are also supplied additional leading questions to ask the children if the child does not know how to respond, or has trouble responding.

## Psychometric Quality

The instrument measures seven subscales. The reliability for each subscale varied somewhat. For 5 of the subscales, the internal consistency was good ($\alpha \geq 0.80$), for one scale, it was moderate ($\alpha = 0.69$) and for one it was marginal ($\alpha = 0.54$) (Ernst, Cookus, & Moravec, 2000). In terms of validity, the inter-correlations of the subscales were low to moderate, indicating that the subscales were not measuring the same thing. Additionally, a discriminant analysis indicated that the instrument could significantly discriminate among the diagnostic categories. Lastly, the scale was sensitive to changes before

*Figure 5.*

and after hospitalization for a sample of children. The Pictorial Instrument for Children and Adolescents exhibited psychometric quality consistent with other measures used in these contexts.

## Cross-Cultural Use

There was no published research regarding the use or evaluation of the instrument for use in cross-cultural settings. Given the type of images, the greatest concerns would be determining if the contexts provided in the images are applicable across cultures. For example, in Figure 5, there is a boy who is bored. The images in the room with the boy might not be familiar to children in all cultures as toys. Similarly, not all children might recognize the television, especially in the bedroom of a child. However, if the assessment were administered individually in an interview style, this could be addressed through the description of the picture by the interviewer, and adaptations could be made on the fly. These types of adaptations, however, do compromise the standardization of the instrument, as all interviewers might not do the same adaptations, so if there need to be adaptations culturally, those types of clarifications should be standardized. Given that, the instrument may need to be adapted in some way to be administered in different cultures, and its generalization across cultures is in question.

# The Pictorial and Descriptive Interest Inventory

The Pictorial and Descriptive Interest Inventory is at nonverbal assessment of occupational interests consisting of 48 items. It is administered over the Internet and provides information of possible career interests for the test-taker. The test can be taken online free of charge at http://www.careerassessment. eu. Results are provided on the screen and can be emailed to the respondent.

## Description of Tasks

The 48 items contain both images and verbal descriptions of various occupations. The test-taker rates whether the occupation is interesting to them, and whether they believe they would be good at the job. The amount of text is significant, and as such, would still require sufficient literacy to complete the assessment.

*Figure 6.*

## Psychometric Quality

The reliability of the scale was found to be high ($\alpha \geq 0.80$) among elementary, high school, and university samples of students. For validity evidence, a factor analysis recovered the expected structure of the data for interest scales, according to theory (Sverko, Barbarovic, & Medugorac, 2014). Further, the scores on the pictorial instrument correlated strongly with moderately with their counterparts on traditional assessments of interest, indicating good convergent validity evidence. This instrument appears to have acceptable levels of psychometric quality, similar to traditional verbal measures.

## Cross-Cultural Use

This instrument relies heavily on text and includes images really to enhance the text. To use this instrument in different cultures, much adaptation would be required, including the translation of the text. To that end, the appropriateness of the photos included should be evaluated for the particular culture as well. The images are photos, and hence have color, and context, which should be assessed relative to the framework presented in Chapter 2. The focus of the individuals would likely vary across cultures. That said, the importance of the image is limited due to the large amounts of text in the questions as well, which is likely to be more central to the assessment than the photo. No published research regarding the use of the instrument in different cultures was found.

## Pictorial Personality Traits Questionnaire for Children (PPTQ-C)

The Pictorial Personality Trait Questionnaire for Children was developed to be a developmentally appropriate assessment of personality traits for children. The assessment is based on 15 items, with three items measuring each of the 5 dimensions of the Big Five personality measures. The development and description of the instrument can be found in the article published by its creators Mackiewicz and Cieciuch (2016).

## Description of the Tasks

Each item consists of two images, with each image showing a child behaving in a different, but related way. For instance, one image could show a child playing alone, with the other image showing a child playing with other children. The child is asked to determine which child is demonstrating behavior that they typically engage in, and also asks them to rate the frequency with which they exhibit the chosen behavior.

## Psychometric Quality

The reliability for the individual subscales were low, ranging from 0.44 to 0.69. These levels of reliability would be considered unacceptable for most standardized assessments. It could be due to the very few number of items per subscale (3 items). With respect to validity, a confirmatory factor analysis indicated that the factor structure of the data did fit a five-dimensional solution, indicating that the structure of the assessment is appropriate, and is likely measuring what it is intending to measure. When correlating the data to another measure of personality, the correlations between the scores on the pictorial assessment and the standard assessment were high, also indicating good validity. The assessment, therefore, is generally measuring the appropriate constructs, however, the limited number of items may be limiting the reliability of the measures. These low levels of reliability indicate that the tool should not be used to make important decisions.

## Cross Cultural Use

There is no published research regarding the use or evaluation of the instrument for cross-cultural use. The images are black and white line drawings that appear to represent a single culture in terms of skin tone, features, and dress. There is some limited text that would need to be translated; however, the text is relatively simple limiting the burden of translation. The types of contexts presented in the images would need to be evaluated for the culture in which the instrument would be administered. Not all children would necessarily understand the context of the images, making the measurement not valid for those children. The types of images used typify a Western lifestyle, which might not generalize to other cultures.

*Figure 7.*

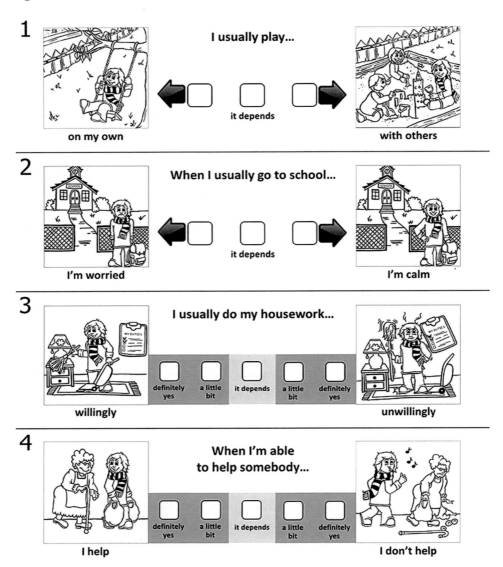

## Pictorial Test of Intelligence

The Pictorial Test of Intelligence is designed to measure general intelligence in children. It includes three subtests including verbal abstractions, form discrimination, and quantitative concepts. Pro-ed is the publisher of this test, and it is commercially available to qualified practitioners. More information about the test and how to order it can be found at http://www.proedinc.com/customer/productView.aspx?ID=783.

## Description of Tasks

The type of tasks that the child is required to respond to depend upon the subscale of the assessment. For Verbal abstractions, the child is presented with a word, or definition of a word, and asked to select a picture that matches what the administrator is saying. Form discrimination tasks require the child to differentiate different geometric figures, or unfinished pictures. Quantitative Concepts are typically not images, but present arithmetic symbols.

## Psychometric Quality

All of the subtests, and the entire battery, demonstrate good reliability ($\alpha \geq 0.88$). Concurrent validity evidence demonstrates moderate to high correlations

*Figure 8.*

with other accepted measures of intelligence (Harper & Tanners, 1974). This psychometric quality indicates that it is acceptable for use with children to measure intelligence.

## Cross-Cultural Use

There was no published research regarding the use or evaluation of the instrument across cultures. It is difficult to assess the potential for use across cultures since images are difficult to obtain. However, given the description of the images, some appear to be similar to the Raven's Progressive Matrices, and all the cautions that were relevant to that assessment would be relevant here. In addition, in the case of children choosing a picture that represents the word provided by the test administrator, this would function well across cultures provided that the words that are included are universally similar across cultures. There are objects and words that would be more or less familiar to children in different cultures and the familiarity with the word would have an effect on the score of the child, so the choice of words included in the assessment would need to be evaluated to determine whether they are appropriate for a given culture.

## PROJECTIVE TESTS

Most projective tests have not been shown to be psychometrically sound. They lack evidence of acceptable reliability or validity. However, clinicians often find that they provide valuable, and valid, information regarding the patients' potential psychopathology, and hence might still be used (Shatz, n.d.). For that reason a sample of the popular projective tests is included here. The purpose of the assessment, and description of the tasks is provided. However, there is not any psychometric quality evidence chosen, as there is little evidence of adequate psychometric quality that has been established.

## Cross-Cultural Use of Projective Assessments

The use of projective tests across cultures might be more straightforward, since there is no "correct" interpretation of the image. Rather, the point of these assessments is to have the respondent provide their own interpretation of the image. In that sense, the details of the image are not relevant. The difficulty instead would come to scoring the assessment, as the responses are usually interpreted with respect to typically responses given by individuals with specific psychological profiles. The need to validate that those set of expected responses in each culture is paramount in using these instruments in other cultures.

## Rorschach Test

The Rorschach Test, or Rorschach Inkblot Test is perhaps the most widely known projective assessment. The purpose of the assessment is to determine the psychological state of the examinee by examining their interpretation of various "inkblots." Because of the ambiguous nature of the inkblots, the patient's psychological state is revealed through how they interpret the image. For those interested in more information including the history and use of the assessment, as well as a view of the images, these can be found at https://www.rorschach.org/index.html.

## Description of Task

The tasks are a series of inkblots that are abstract shapes not intended to represent any obvious object. There are common interpretations of most of the inkblots, however, and the responses of the test taker reveals whether their interpretations are similar to those that have no psychological disturbance.

*Figure 9.*

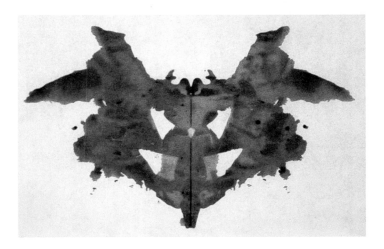

## Thematic Apperception Test

The Thematic Apperception Test (TAT) was designed to identify personality characteristics and potential personality disorders in children and adults. This assessment is published by Pearson and can be ordered at http://www.pearsonclinical.com/psychology/products/100000341/thematic-apperception-test-tat.html. Administration is to be completed by a trained professional. For more detailed information of the test, the interested reader is directed to https://www.mentalhelp.net/articles/psychological-testing-thematic-apperception-test/.

## Description of Tasks

The patient is presented black and white different scenes, and is asked to construct a story about what they see in the picture. Typically 20 scenes are presented to the child to elicit their stories.

It is clear that while these assessments use images rather than text, they are not necessarily more exciting or engaging than text-based assessments. They do, however, harness the power of using imagery for eliciting responses in a way that is different than text. And most of these assessments have been

*Figure 10.*

shown to be psychometrically sound. They are the foundation on which we can build these newer, engaging assessments. To that end, there have been two successful attempts to develop image-based assessments that do capitalize in the visual engagement aspects of the Internet quizzes. These assessments are discussed next.

# NEXT GENERATION ASSESSMENTS

These types of assessment are the type that is new, cutting edge, visually engaging and most like the popular Internet quizzes. These assessments are more current assessments that can be found on the Internet to measure psychological attributes or interests. The Internet quizzes are not included here, as they are mostly non-scientific, and while data are collected and used, there is not enough public information to know anything about the quality of these quizzes, although it would be quite interesting to investigate. However, there are a limited number of visual assessments that are used in a more professional context, and those products are reviewed here. These assessments are most similar to the assessments that are of interest in this book, and as such, more detailed information is provided for these assessments.

## Visual DNA

Visual DNA is a company that creates image-based quizzes to use to assess personality characteristics for individuals to understand themselves better, as well as to allow businesses to serve their customers better (https://www.visualdna.com/about/). The company offers two different quizzes on their website:

- Who Am I?
- Personality Quiz

These quizzes, as they referred to them, are described as visual questionnaires, and while visuals do play a large role in these quizzes, they differ somewhat from the conceptualization of the visual assessments as have been discussed so far. These visual questionnaires are not devoid of text, nor are there attempts to eliminate text from the quizzes. The nature of the items in these quizzes is that the question is provided in text, and the response options are images. As is shown in the example in Figure 11, a

*Figure 11.*

## Which of these amazes you most?

Pick one to start

question from the Who Am I? quiz might be "Which of these amazes you the most?" The answer options are five pictures, and the respondent chooses the one that amazes them the most.

An example from the Personality Quiz is similar, where the question is text-based, and the responses are images. In some cases, the responses are not even images, but are also text, as illustrated in Figure 12

While these assessments clearly incorporate images, they are not using images to necessarily avoid the use of text, as previous examples have done. The images undoubtedly enhance the quality of the assessment, as the images still evoke feelings that would be difficult to evoke with text, and the engagement with the instrument is likely higher. Thus, it is not to be dismissive of these types of visual questionnaires, just to highlight the differences between visual questionnaires like this, and those that seek to limit the use of text, to gain the advantages presented in Chapter 1.

Each of these is an image-based quiz that takes about 10 minutes to complete. You get a dominant personality label (e.g. "Seeker") and subscores. Some of the subscores connect to more traditional personality measures, like the Big 5, while others do not (e.g. "Seeker"). Feedback is given to the individual immediately after completing the quiz.

*Figure 12.*

Which of these amazes you most?

The tone of the feedback provided to the person taking the quiz is not what is typically expected. As a professional company, the tone of the feedback is more informal than might be expected. As examples, the following feedback might be received:

- "You really live life on the edge...of your easy chair"
- "We could tell you to reimagine your long-term goals (do you have them?), understand the wider impact of your decisions (did you make any?), but really you need to stop sweating it and (try to) be cool."

While it is clear that the tone is meant to be light and fun, depending on the individual, the tone of this type of feedback might be undesirable, and could have a negative impact on their feelings about the results of the quizzes. This type of feedback might appeal to the new generation of media savvy, social media consumers. The quizzes are not marketed as being just for fun, but to help the user gain insight into themselves. For example, from the homepage of the quizzes, the website states, "A free visual quiz to help you understand yourself."

## Applications of the Assessments

Visual DNA appeals to business through marketing efforts. For example, they use the image-based personality measures to enhance market segmentation. Using the results of the personality measures, companies can have a better understanding of who their customers are, thus they can more accurately target their segment of the market, and make advertising more personal and relevant to their customers. This should aid in growing their customer base. Most specifically, they can refine their understanding of who their best customers are; that is, what are the personality traits of their best customers, which will enable targeting their customer base more specifically. Advertising can be more effectively targeted to meet the emotional characteristics of the desired audience.

## Psychometric Quality

There was very little specific information regarding the psychometric quality of the quizzes. There was a white paper available online that discussed their methodologies used to analyze the data, however, the results of those analyses were not available. As an exception, there was one validity study that examined the correlation between the scores on the five personality subscales of the "Big Five" personality measure, and traditional measures of personality. The correlations presented indicated evidence of convergent validity, with strong correlations for all five subscales, ranging from 0.56 to 0.75, with most of the correlations closer to 0.70, which often signifies strong convergent validity evidence (Chamorro-Premuzic & Ahmetoglu, 2013). These quizzes are probably of good psychometric quality, however, there is little data that is made publicly available.

## Cross-Cultural Use

Visual DNA does not report any use of their products in different cultures. The documentation on their product relies on the research on the Big Five Inventory as being generalizable across cultures, and assumes the same property of their own product. However, this may not be true, given that the design of the traditional assessment and the image-based assessment are vastly different. Additionally, the Big Five Inventory does have some problems generalizing to Eastern Asian cultures (see Chapter 5). More work to study how well it functions is warranted, as it is an internet-based product. It appears to be only administered in English, and there is a text component to the assessment, and as such, would only be relevant for English speaking people. However, being English speaking does not mean that there aren't cultural aspects to how the images presented would be interpreted. The images are highly engaging, full color photos. All of the features of images that are affected by culture would need to be explored, as all images contain color, have context attached to them. The positive is that there is very little extraneous background information in many of the photos, with close ups on the parts of the images that are of central importance.

## Traitify

In addition to VisualDNA, the other large company making image-based assessments online is Traitify. This company customizes image-based assessments for their clients that present the test taker with an image, and they respond to the image as "me" or "not me." They offer six "off-the-shelf" quizzes as well as a custom personality measure. For each quiz, they provide a list of contexts that each quiz is appropriate for. The six products that are readily available are:

- **Careers:** For Career recommendation, college planning, career counseling
- **Core:** Dating, content curation
- **Heroes:** Comic book recommendations, nerdy dating, superhero marketing, curated nerd culture content
- **Movie:** Film/TV recommendations
- **Persuasion:** Identify management potential, supplement to career assessment
- **Intro/Extro:** Supplement to career assessment

These assessments definitely attempt to minimize the use of text in the assessments, although there is text to supplement the images. The respondent is asked to rate an image as "like me" and "not like me" and the text on the image helps the respondent to understand the context in which the image is to be interpreted. For example, one question presents an image of a younger hand reaching out to hold the hand of an older person. The respondent is to indicate if this image is "like me" or "not like me." There are multiple interpretations of what this image might be trying to elicit in the responder. For example, the respondent might answer this question in terms of if they have close relationships with elderly people, like their grandparents. The text provided on the image is "Caring for Others." A copy of this image is provided in Figure 13.

*Figure 13.*

This text helps the respondent understand the context for interpreting the image. They can respond to either the text alone, the image alone, or, most likely, the combination of the image and the text. The use of both the image and the text is likely very powerful. The simplicity of the text is also a feature, where the requirements for literacy are kept to a minimum. Although assessments of this type would still require translation, at least the nature of the text is far less complex than that found in the typical text-based assessment.

The feedback provided to the user is quite informative and presented in a visually appealing way. An example of the results from the Career Personality Assessment is provided in Figure 14. A graphical representation of the dominant traits of the user is provided along with a description of these personality traits.

## Applications of the Assessments

Traitify has been quite successful in marketing their product for use in many applications. Traitify has launched itself with using their image-based personality assessments in many contexts that are exciting, and in ways that

*Figure 14.*

**Careers Assessment Results**

   PERSONALITY BLEND

## Analyzer/Visionary

You are drawn to others who share your interest and curiosity in the world. A natural leader and full of ambition, you're often the one presenting the paper others have come to hear. Others look up to you and follow your lead. You are a deep thinker, and you enjoy learning new things. You also always have a suggestion for something new that you want to check out or learn about, and your friends appreciate getting new ideas from you. You are happiest when surrounded by other people, and you thrive out in the world. However, you also enjoy a quiet evening at home with several close friends full of invigorating discussion and deep thinking.

traditional assessments have not been used as widely. These opportunities provide for some innovative ways to use assessments, and image-based assessments offer many advantages because they are more fun, engaging, and easy to complete and score on the fly. Since there aren't a lot of these types of assessments in use currently outside of typical assessment contexts, these examples rely heavily on those administered by Traitify. Some of these examples are highlighted here, and for more detailed information, the reader is directed to www.traitify.com.

Hiring and team building within a company is an application of these image-based assessments that Traitify has strongly developed. Their products make the personality data accessible and actionable by their clients. While traditional assessments of personality could be used in a similar way, the time it would take to administer, score and then interpret the data would be extensive. The typical user takes approximately 90 seconds to complete one of Traitify's personality assessments (Traitify, ND). With this level of efficiency, it is easy to gather the data on all current and future employees. These data can then be made actionable in various ways. For example, personality types for all employees could be broken down into the various categories provided by Traitify, such as "Planner," "Action-Taker," "Analyzer," "Visionary," "Mentor," "Inventor," and "Naturalist." These categories also come with descriptions of what traits people in each of those categories possess. The number of employees of each type can be provided, as is shown in Figure 15.

This type of information can help inform the company about which types are most successful, which types are not well represented currently, and

*Figure 15.*

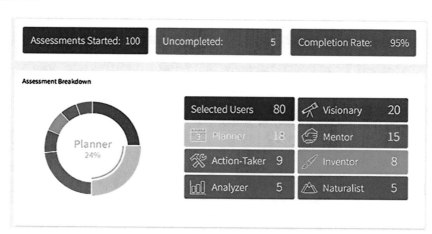

which types might need to be hired. Additionally, these types could be used to create different types of teams. To accomplish this goal, Traitify provides profiles of people on teams to see how different employees align with respect to personality traits to be sure team members don't clash. This is represented in Figure 16.

The last example provided by the company is the use of the assessment to look at the culture of the organization, or team. Since organizational culture and personality need to match for ideal employer-employee satisfaction, the culture of the organization can be assessed by considering the traits of the successful employees. This type of analysis could result in the following type of data presented in Figure 17.

Beyond business applications for hiring, Traitify has created solutions around entertainment and leisure. Through their personality assessments, people can be matched to particular movies that they might like, for example. These personality assessments can be accessed through a mobile application, and result in a type of moviegoer that someone might be: Believer, Dramatic,

*Figure 16.*

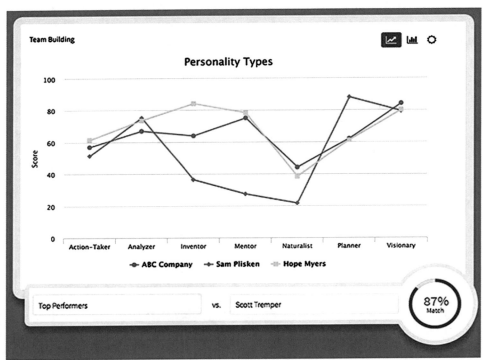

*Figure 17.*

Indie, Laughaholic, Nail Biter, Romantic, or Stunt Double. These results can help the user choose movies that they might like, or even to see if they are compatible with a person that they might like to go to the movies with! The app is free.

Some of the products that were developed by Woofound, which was the previous name of Traitify, appear to no longer exist, but were quite innovative and interesting, so are presented here as potential applications of image-based assessments. There were two products developed by Woofound: Woofound Explore, and Woofound Compass. Aspects of these products remain in Traitify products, but it is not clear if these particular exact products exist.

Woofound Explore was a mobile app that gave the user a series of images that were rated as "Me" or "Not Me." The assessment took less than a minute. The user was then matched with things to do in over 70 different cities, which were matched to the users preferences. Woofound claimed that their results were 92 percent reliable (http://wildabouttravel.boardingarea.com/2013/09/7199/),

Woofound Compass was a product that matched students in Universities to courses, on-campus activities, clubs and ultimately careers that would match the student's interests and personality type.

## Psychometric Quality

The psychometric quality information on the assessments is provided in a white paper on their website. It appears as though the psychometric information is related to the Career Personality Assessment, which consists of 56 images that the respondents rate. The reliability of this assessment was assessed using 482 respondents, and was determined to have a coefficient alpha of 0.94, which is quite high. This assessment is clearly quite reliable. The assessment is designed to measure seven personality types, and the reliability for each type is also provided, and was high for all of the types ($\alpha \geq 0.90$). The validity evidence included an analysis of the factor structure of the career assessment that they develop does indicate that the structure of the assessment aligns with the theoretical structure around personality types, although the information related to the analyses were limited. This company appears to be dedicated to producing high quality assessments to provide guidance for their users, and clients.

## Cross-Cultural Use

Similar to VisualDNA, there is little information available regarding the use of the instrument across different cultures, although it appears only an English language version is available, and all items include text as well as images. Similar to VisualDNA, the images are colorful, highly engaging, and would thus need to be scrutinized for use in different cultures, should that be desired. All of the features that can be affected by culture (focus, color, etc.) would need to be assessed in these images.

## SUMMARY

This chapter provided an overview of a sample of visual assessments that have been used over a long period of time, and have been carefully created and validated. It also provided examples of newer, less researched visual assessments. It is clear that there is a difference between the types of visual assessments that have been historically used, that have had to rely on reproduction in print, rather than rendering on a computer screen. In the more traditional visual assessments, color could not be used, as it would have been cost prohibitive to print large volumes in an economical way. The newer assessments have no intention of being delivered in a hard copy format, making the use of more vivid images possible. These examples highlight how the use of technology can increase the quality of images that can be used, and increase the level of engagement with the instrument. The prospect of using technology makes the use of visual assessments even more promising.

The possibility of using these assessments across cultures was also explored for each assessment. While the newer assessments were more engaging than the older assessments, due to the availability of technology, the use of full color photos also increases the complexity of using the assessments in different cultures.

# REFERENCES

Achenbach, T. M., & Rescorla, L. A. (2001). *Manual for the ASEBA School-Age Forms and Profiles*. Burlington, VT: University of Vermont, Research Center for Children, Youth, and Families.

Benson. (2003). Intelligence across cultures. *Monitor on Psychology, 34*(2), 56.

Brouwers, S. A., Van de Vijver, F. J. R., & Hemert, D. A. (2009). Variation in Ravens Progressive Matrices scores across time and place. *Learning and Individual Differences, 19*(3), 330–338. doi:10.1016/j.lindif.2008.10.006

Chamorro-Premuzic, T., & Ahmetoglu, G. (2013). *Personality 101*. Springer.

Domino, G., & Domino, M. L. (2006). *Psychological Testing: An Introduction*. Cambridge University Press.

Dubi, K., & Schneider, S. (2009). The Picture Anxiety Test (PAT): A new pictorial assessment of anxiety symptoms in young children. *Journal of Anxiety Disorders, 23*(8), 1148–1157. doi:10.1016/j.janxdis.2009.07.020 PMID:19709849

Ernst, M., Cookus, B. A., & Moravec, B. C. (2000). Pictorial instrument for children and adolescents. *Journal of the American Academy of Child and Adolescent Psychiatry, 39*(1), 94–99. doi:10.1097/00004583-200001000-00021 PMID:10638072

Harpers, D. C., & Tanners, H. (1974). The French pictorial test of intelligence and the Stanford-Binet L-M: A concurrent validity study with physically impaired children. *The Clinical Psychologist, 30*(2), 178–180. doi:10.1002/1097-4679(197404)30:2<178::AID-JCLP2270300216>3.0.CO;2-O PMID:4281002

Kuiper, N. A., Grimshaw, M., Leite, C., & Kirsh, G. (2004). Humor is not always the best medicine: Specific components of sense of humor and psychological well-being. *Humor: International Journal of Humor Research, 17*(1-2), 135–168. doi:10.1515/humr.2004.002

Leiner, M., Rescorla, L., Medina, I., Blanc, O., & Ortiz, M. (2009). Psychometric comparisons of the pictorial behavior checklist with the standard version of the instrument. *Psychological Assessment, 22*(3), 618–627. doi:10.1037/a0019778 PMID:20822274

Linares Scott, T.J., Short, E.J., Singer, L.T., Russ, S.W., & Minnes, S. (2006). Psychometric properties of the Dominic interactive Assessment, A Computerized Self-report for Children. *Assessment, 13*(1), 16-26.

Mackiewicz, M., & Cieciuch, J. (2016). Pictorial Personality Traits Questionnaire for Children (PPTQ-C)- A new measure of children's personality traits. *Frontiers in Psychology.* https://doi.org/10.3389/fpsyg.2016.00498

Shatz, P. (n.d.). *Projective personality testing: Psychological testing.* Retrieved November 21, 2012, from Saint Joseph's University, Department of Psychology: http://schatz.sju.edu/intro/1001lowfi/personality/projectiveppt/sld001.htm

Shojaei, T., Wazana, A., Pitrou, I., Gilbert, F., Bergeron, L., Valla, J. P., & Kovess-Masfety, V. (2009). Psychometric properties of the Dominic Interactive in a large French sample. *Canadian Journal of Psychiatry, 54*(11), 767–776. doi:10.1177/070674370905401107 PMID:19961665

Sverko, I., Barbarovic, T., & Medugorac, V. (2014). Pictorial assessment of interest: Development and evaluation of pictorial and descriptive Interest Inventory. *Journal of Vocational Behavior, 84*(3), 356–366. doi:10.1016/j.jvb.2014.02.008

Valla, J.-P., Bergeron, L., & Smolla, N. (2000). The Dominic-R: A pictorial interview for 6- to 11-year old children. *Journal of the American Academy of Child and Adolescent Psychiatry, 39*(1), 85–93. doi:10.1097/00004583-200001000-00020 PMID:10638071

Yates, T. (1990). Theories of cognitive development. In M. Lewis (Ed.), *Child and Adolescent Psychiatry* (pp. 109–129). Baltimore, MD: Williams & Wilkins.

# Chapter 4
# Determining Equivalence of Measures Across Cultures

## ABSTRACT

*Chapter 4 considers how the equivalence of measures is determined across different cultural groups. Equivalence of measures in this instance refers to whether or not the assessment means the same thing across those different cultures. The types of bias that might exist as well as methods used to assess potential bias are described. These ideas are presented for assessments in general, and are not limited to visual assessments. Examples from the literature are provided to illustrate the methods discussed in this chapter. Application to visual assessment is also discussed at the conclusion of the chapter.*

## INTRODUCTION

Assessments are often given across multiple cultural, ethnic or language groups. The reasons for cross-cultural assessment vary; in some cases, there is a desire to compare results of assessments across different cultural groups, while other times, there is efficiency to using a pre-existing instrument instead of developing a new one. While the specific issues might vary in these two contexts, great care is needed to understand what the assessments means in each culture, and whether or not the assessment means the same thing across those different cultures. When scores are being compared, it is essential that the scores mean the same thing, so that we aren't comparing apples to oranges. When an instrument is adapted from one culture to another, without the goal

DOI: 10.4018/978-1-5225-2691-9.ch004

of comparison, it may not be crucial that the sores are comparable, however, if the scores are not comparable, understanding what the scores mean and represent in the particular context is necessary. There is a wealth of research in the field of psychometrics that centers on evaluating the cross-cultural equivalence of assessments.

Van de Vijver and Tanzer (2004) present a framework for thinking about the equivalence of scores across cultures. They define equivalence as a lack of bias in the measure, and identify three sources of bias:

- Construct Bias occurs if the construct that is being measured is not identical across cultures.
- Method bias, which consists of sample bias, instrument bias, and administration bias. Sample bias occurs when the samples are not comparable on characteristics other than the target construct, which may influence the construct. Instrument bias occurs when one group is less familiar with the type of questions being administered than the other group, leading to score differences that are artifacts of the familiarity of the testing conditions. Lastly, administration bias occurs when communication differences occur, say between an interviewer and interviewee with different language or cultural backgrounds.
- Item bias, or differential item functioning: item bias occurs at the item level, when items have different meaning across the cultural groups.

Depending on the context, the types of bias that need to be evaluated should be determined. Van de Vijver and Tanzer (2004) present some strategies for dealing with each type of bias. An excerpt of that is provided in Table 1.

*Table 1. Types of bias and strategies to address each*

| Type of Bias | Strategies |
|---|---|
| Construct | 1. Develop measure simultaneously in multiple cultures.<br>2. Develop measure in each culture separately, and then administer them across the multiple cultures<br>3. Use experts that span all cultures in the development<br>4. Use samples of examinees from multiple cultures<br>5. Conduct think aloud protocols across cultures<br>6. Convergent/discriminant validity studies |
| Method | 1. Detailed training of administrators<br>2. Detailed instructions for administration<br>3. Assessment of response styles of examinees |
| Item | 1. Judgmental review of items<br>2. Differential item functioning analyses<br>3. Distractor analyses |

In the context of a visual assessment, most of these types of bias apply. For construct validity, all six of these strategies would be useful and should be applied where possible. For most people, method bias is less likely to be an issue than the other types of bias, since these assessments will be familiar to people with access to the Internet. In cultures where access to Internet or computers might be limited, then method bias becomes more of a concern, and it would be necessary to train the respondents on the type of assessment. Item bias would be a very important area to assess, especially in these early phases of visual assessments, where the functioning of items might not be well understood. Judgmental review of the items, strategy one, would be especially useful when addressing potential item bias, to review features of items that might not translate well across cultures. Strategy two, differential item functioning analyses, is likewise important to ascertain which items are performing differently across cultures. Depending on the format of the assessment, a distractor analysis (strategy three) may or may not be relevant, just as with a text-based assessment.

When reviewing the literature the research has focused on construct bias and item bias, with no studies being identified that have addressed method bias. A summary of the types of studies done within construct bias and item bias is provided.

## Construct Bias

There is a large body of research dedicated to the assessment of construct bias in assessments that are administered in multiple cultures. In these studies, the focus has been on examining the factor structure of the assessment across various cultures. These studies would be included as convergent validity studies. Within these papers, various methods were explored to assess the equivalence of the factor structure across cultures. These methods are reviewed here, and are broken into two categories: exploratory analyses, and measurement invariance.

## EXPLORATORY ANALYSES

There are relatively few exploratory methods used for the purpose of examining the similarity of the construct between assessments administered to different cultures. It is not common to use exploratory methods when comparing factor structures, because exploratory procedures imply that there is not a theoretical structure that exists, rather it is an attempt to identify the underlying factor structure that might exist. Therefore, in contexts where there is a hypothesized factor structure, it is more common to use confirmatory methods to determine whether or not that structure can reasonably hold in the sample of data. Exploratory methods are more susceptible to explaining "noise" in the data, or random error. This is especially true with Principle Components Analysis, as compared to Exploratory Factor Analysis, where an attempt to remove measurement error is made.

Two studies that were found that utilized exploratory methods. One used Principle Components Analysis (Weiss & Burger, 2006) and the second used Exploratory Factor Analysis (Creed, Patton, & Watson, 2002). Weiss and Burger (2006) used principle components analysis to compare the factor structure of a measure adapted into a second language. While the core 3 factors were found in the adapted measure, the exact factor structure was not replicated between the two forms of the measure. The lack of consistency might be a result of using exploratory method, especially Principal Components Analysis. If a confirmatory process were used, it may have been found that the desired structure had acceptable fit to the data.

The Creed, Patton, and Watson (2002) study examined the factor structure of a measure administered to three different cultural groups. While the same number of factors was extracted across the versions of the measure, the factors did not appear to align with one another. Again, it is difficult to know whether a common factor structure might exist without doing a confirmatory procedure.

## MEASUREMENT INVARIANCE

Measurement invariance is often thought of as the same thing as construct bias, as defined above, along with item bias. Measurement invariance applies when a construct is measured in the same way across different groups of people. It also applies when the items measure the construct in the same way. There are many types of measurement invariance, with differing levels of strength of invariance depending on the type of invariance being studied. The details of measurement invariance are beyond the scope of this book, but the interested reader is directed to the following references (e.g., Milfont & Fischer, 2010). Presented here is more of a conceptual idea about measurement invariance.

If you imagine that there is a factor structure that represents the construct of interest, the goal is to determine whether or not that factor structure is the same across the different versions of the measure. Each of the items of the instrument is related to the measures of the factor that they are associated with. So, if there is a 10 item scale, with the first five items measuring one latent factor, $n_1$, and the second five items measuring the second latent factor, $n_2$, you can see that each item is an observation related to its specific factor, as shown in Figure 1. Along each arrow is a value $f_i$, which represents a factor loading. The factor loading quantifies the relationship between the observed item and the latent factor it is associated with.

What it means for the structure to be the same across versions of an instrument is not necessarily straightforward, and can exist at multiple levels. Factorial invariance states that the same factors underlie the construct in all groups. That is, the model shown in Figure 1 fits for all groups of interest.

*Figure 1.*

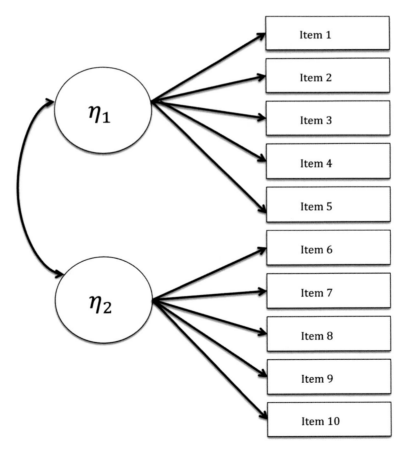

This is a basic form of invariance, and is what the exploratory procedures above are essentially trying to investigate. Then, one can determine if the relationship between the items and the factors themselves (i.e. factor loadings) is the same across the versions of the instrument (weak factorial invariance). This type of invariance implies that the same latent variables, or constructs, are being measured similarly in the different groups.

We can go beyond whether or not the same constructs are being measured to investigating whether differences in means can be accurately compared across the different forms, if we wish. By making further constraints on the model, we can ensure that changes in the means of observed variables (items) indicate mean changes in the construct. When the structure of the data of the groups allows for this type of constraint to hold, we achieve strong factorial invariance. Lastly, in strict factorial invariance, we can be sure that the error variance of the measures across the different groups are also invariant, or equal. This is a stronger form of measurement invariance.

In practice, it is not typical to find strict factorial invariance. It is not always easy to even find weak factorial invariances. Sometimes, the relationships of items to constructs are the same for some items across groups, but not others. This can be referred to as partial invariance. If partial invariance is obtained, one can either try to modify items, delete items, etc. to achieve a subset of items that exhibit greater levels of invariance. However, those choices might be dependent on the sample of data that is being used, and might not hold over other samples of data.

The exploration of measurement invariance is one of the most popular methods of assessing construct bias in the literature. These analyses can be applied with either confirmatory factor analysis or structural equation modeling. The majority of studies applied confirmatory factor analysis (Bieda, Hirschfeld, Schönfeld, Brailovskaia, Zhang, & Margraf, 2016; Furukawa, Streiner, Azuma, Higuchi, Kamijima, Kanba, & Miura, 2005; Liu, Millsap, West, Tein, Tanaka, & Grimm, 2016; Luk, King, McCarty, Vander Stoep, & McCauley, 2016; Wasti, Tan, Brower, & Önder, 2007; Wu, Lu, Tan, Yao, Steca, Abela, & Hankin, 2012; Whisman & Judd, 2016; Xu, Hilpert, Randall, Li, & Bodenmann, 2016).

A popular approach to measurement invariance with confirmatory factor analysis is the multiple-group analysis (Bieda, Hirschfeld, Schönfeld, Brailovskaia, Zhang, & Margraf, 2016; Liu, Millsap, West, Tein, Tanaka, & Grimm, 2016; Luk, King, McCarty, Vander Stoep, & McCauley, 2016; Wu, Lu, Tan, Yao, Steca, Abela, & Hankin, 2012; Wasti, Tan, Brower, & Önder,

2007; Whisman & Judd, 2016). Given its popularity, some attention is given to this approach. In the multiple group analysis, the first step is to identify a confirmatory factor model that fits in all groups separately. This model will look like the model in Figure 1, with the appropriate number of factors and items, of course. Once this model is specified separately for each group, the model is fit to the groups together in one model, with all parameters free to vary from group to group. Once that model is fit, then the next step is to fix the factor loadings, (the $f_i$ in the figure) to be equal in each group, to determine if the factor loadings are the same across groups, indicting weak factorial invariance. Then, lastly, fix the intercepts across groups as well as the factor loadings across groups to test for strict invariance. This approach is straightforward, and allows for testing for invariance in a very complete way. The disadvantage to the model is that there are many parameters to estimate, which means that the sample size requirement for all groups is large. Additionally, when there are many groups, it is difficult to carry out these analyses. Because of these requirements, many people will opt for a simpler analysis, sacrificing the ability to test for the equality of so many parameters. A popular competing model is the multiple-indicators, multiple-causes (MIMIC) models, which will be discussed later in this chapter.

Due to the large number of studies, each study will not be reviewed individually; rather, common themes among the articles will be highlighted.

While there were a few studies that confirmed a consistent structure across the different forms of the measures, most of the studies concluded that while there were similarities across forms, there were small to moderate differences as well, and indicated partial measurement invariance. The particulars of the differences depended on the constructs being measured, the quality of the instruments, etc. However, across all of these variables, it is clear that there appears to be partial invariance when looking at instruments across cultures. It is a wonder if strict invariance can be met. That does not mean that it is not possible to use assessment across cultures, but that the standard of strict invariance might be difficult to meet in practice. Since most assessments used cross-culturally demonstrate partial invariance, which might be sufficient for use of assessments in practice, with the understanding that there is not perfect invariance between the assessments, adding an additional source of error to the scores.

There were some articles that utilized structural equation modeling. Two recent studies illustrated how structural equation modeling could be utilized for cross-cultural assessments (Byrne & van de Vijver, 2010; Yuan & Chan,

2016). Again, while there wasn't necessarily strict factorial invariance, the level of invariance observed was sufficient for the authors to warrant the use of the instruments across cultures.

## ITEM BIAS

There are many papers that have examined item bias across instruments adapted for other cultures. Typically these analyses are in the form of differential item functioning (DIF) studies. In DIF studies, respondents are matched to have the same level of the latent trait (i.e. construct) and differences in item responses are compared to see if there are systematic differences between how cultures respond to individual items. In this way, items can be flagged as potentially being interpreted differently across cultures. There are a plethora of DIF techniques available. Several recent studies were examined, and there were no consistent methodologies employed (Kankaraš & Moors, 2014; Kim, Cohen, & Park, 1995; Kulas, Thompson, & Anderson, 2011; Yildirim & Berberoglu, 2009). A promising method for examining DIF with a measurement invariance approach is the use of the multiple-indicator multiple-causes model (MIMIC) model (Woods, 2009). The MIMIC model is also called confirmatory factor analysis with covariates, since it is using a confirmatory factor analysis approach while incorporating the covariate of country. Using the example of shown in 4.1 as the CFA model for two countries, once this model is shown to fit adequately in both cultures, the covariate of country is added, as depicted in Figure 2.

Notice that in this model, country has an effect on the responses to the images only indirectly in that it has an effect on the latent variables, which in turn, are responsible for the responses to the images. This model is then tested, and if it shows acceptable fit, then the third model can be fit to the data. In the third model, shown in Figure 3, a direct effect is added to the model between the covariate of country, and one of the images, say item 10. This direct effect is depicted as a dotted arrow between the country and the image.

This direct effect means that the country that the respondent lives in has a direct effect on the response to the image, which cannot be accounted for by the latent variable. That is to say, there is something about living in a particular country that has an influence on how you respond to the images. If this effect is significant, it means that there is differential response to the images based on which country you live in, even when your level of the latent trait is the same. This significant effect is a measure of differential item

*Figure 2.*

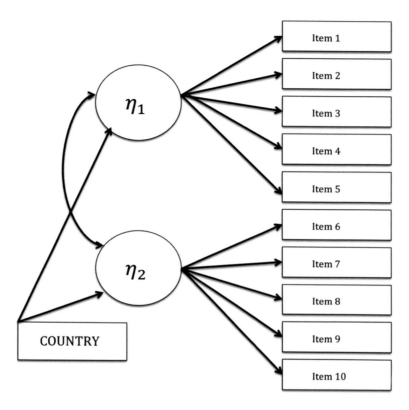

functioning, or DIF. When DIF is present, measurement invariance does not hold, and the image that exhibits DIF would not be generalizable across the different countries, or cultures.

Once items are identified as exhibiting DIF, an attempt is made to try to understand why the DIF was observed. Is something actually functioning differently between cultures? Or is it a statistical artifact? Once DIF is detected, what do you do? These questions are not simple. It is often difficult to know where the DIF comes from, and so the consequences of the DIF must be explored. If retaining the items would make the inferences about groups incorrect, then removing the items would make more sense. How to make the determination is difficult. However, in the context of cross-cultural assessment, the presence of DIF means that the item is not functioning the same way in the two different cultures, and using that item may compromise the comparability of scores across cultures.

*Figure 3.*

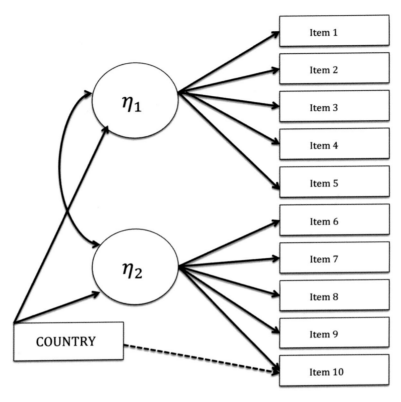

## APPLICATIONS TO VISUAL ASSESSMENTS

The issues of cross-cultural assessment apply to visual assessments just as they do to text-based assessments. The difference is in the need to translate, or adapt the test to fit the language of the other culture. Many of the issues in adapting, or translating, an instrument to be used in a different culture stems from the lack of consistent language across cultures, and what that language means. Without the use of language, the hope is that the use of visual assessments across different cultures is more straightforward. It is true that it must be ascertained that the construct is still the same, and that the items are free from bias, however, the hope is that it is easier to do that by finding images that might be more free from cultural interpretation than language. The challenge then becomes determining whether or not the images mean the same things across different cultures. It is known that certain hand gestures are not invariant across cultures, with the same gesture being positive in one culture and offensive in another (Cotton, 2013). Due to these cultural differences, it is important to assess that the images have the same meaning across cultures if one is to use a visual assessment in different countries. Fortunately, the techniques that are used to detect problematic items in text-based assessments can be applied in the same way to image-based assessments, or items. As such, the machinery and psychometrics are the same regardless of the type of assessment; the promise of the visual assessment over the text-based assessment is that it would be easier to identify images that transcend culture than it is to translate text across languages and cultures.

## SUMMARY

When using assessments across multiple cultures, it is imperative that attention be paid to all aspects of bias that could potentially threaten the validity of the use of the scores across cultures. Since the goal of using a common instrument across multiple cultures would be to have scores that are comparable, attention to the issues of measurement invariance are critical. Without investigating the cross-cultural equivalence of the scores, it would be impossible to make any comparisons of the scores that were meaningful. Attending to, and addressing any potential biases can allow for the use of the scores across cultures in a valid way.

The next chapter illustrates the construction of a visual assessment, and includes the steps mentioned in this chapter to handle the potential biases that might arise when creating an assessment across two cultures.

Constructing any assessment that is to be used across cultures has the potential to result in cultural bias in the assessment questions. There are multiple types of bias that can occur, including construct, method, and item bias. Procedures exist to limit the inclusion of bias in the questions, and these

*Figure 4.*

Take Home Tips
When making cross-cultural assessment be sure to address:
- Construct Equivalence: the test measures the same thing in all cultures in which it is being used
- Method Bias: Make sure administrators/respondents understand the format
- Item Bias: Item responses don't depend on culture, only on construct being measured

should be employed as much as possible. After the assessment has been constructed, the extent to which these types of bias exist should be evaluated. Many different types of analyses exist to do so. These types of analysis are commonly referred to as measurement invariance broadly, or differential item functioning, which is a type of measurement invariance. When used in the context of image-based assessments, there are some differences due to the fact that there is no text to translate, which simplifies the process to some extent, as there is no bias introduced through the translation of text. However, as discussed in Chapter 2, there are cultural implications of specific image features that should be attended to.

# REFERENCES

Bieda, A., Hirschfeld, G., Schönfeld, P., Brailovskaia, J., Zhang, X. C., & Margraf, J. (2016). Universal happiness? Cross-cultural measurement invariance of scales assessing positive mental health. *Psychological Assessment*. doi:10.1037/pas0000353 PMID:27322203

Byrne, B. M., & van de Vijver, F. R. (2010). Testing for Measurement and Structural Equivalence in Large-Scale Cross-Cultural Studies: Addressing the Issue of Nonequivalence. *International Journal of Testing*, *10*(2), 107–132. doi:10.1080/15305051003637306

Creed, P. A., Patton, W., & Watson, M. B. (2002). Cross-Cultural equivalence of the Career Decision-Making Self-Efficacy Scale-Short Form: An Australian and South African comparison. *Journal of Career Assessment*, *10*(3), 327–342. doi:10.1177/10672702010003004

Furukawa, T. A., Streiner, D. L., Azuma, H., Higuchi, T., Kamijima, K., Kanba, S., & Miura, S. et al. (2005). Cross-cultural equivalence in depression assessment: Japan-Europe-North American study. *Acta Psychiatrica Scandinavica*, *112*(4), 279–285. doi:10.1111/j.1600-0447.2005.00587.x PMID:16156835

Kankaraš, M., & Moors, G. (2014). Analysis of cross-cultural comparability of pisa 2009 scores. *Journal of Cross-Cultural Psychology*, *45*(3), 381–399. doi:10.1177/0022022113511297

Kim, S. H., Cohen, A. S., & Park, T. H. (1995). Detection of differential item functioning in multiple groups. *Journal of Educational Measurement*, *32*(3), 261–276. doi:10.1111/j.1745-3984.1995.tb00466.x

Kulas, J. T., Thompson, R. C., & Anderson, M. G. (2011). California Psychological Inventory Dominance Scale measurement equivalence: General population Normative and Indian, U.K., and U.S. managerial samples. *Educational and Psychological Measurement*, *71*(1), 245–257. doi:10.1177/0013164410391580

Liu, Y., Millsap, R. E., West, S. G., Tein, J., Tanaka, R., & Grimm, K. J. (2016). Testing measurement invariance in longitudinal data with ordered-categorical measures. *Psychological Methods*. doi:10.1037/met0000075 PMID:27213981

Luk, J. W., King, K. M., McCarty, C. A., Vander Stoep, A., & McCauley, E. (2016). Measurement invariance testing of a three-factor model of parental warmth, psychological control, and knowledge across European and Asian/Pacific Islander American youth. *Asian American Journal of Psychology*, *7*(2), 97–107. doi:10.1037/aap0000040 PMID:27347358

Milfont, T. L., & Fischer, R. (2010). Testing measurement invariance across groups: Applications in cross-cultural research. *International Journal of Psychological Research*, *3*(1), 111–121.

Van de Vijver, F., & Tanzer, N. (2004). Bias and equivalence in cross-cultural assessment: an overview. *Revue europeenne de psychologie appliquee, 54*, 119-135.

Wasti, S. A., Tan, H. H., Brower, H. H., & Önder, Ç. (2007). Cross-cultural measurement of supervisor trustworthiness: An assessment of measurement invariance across three cultures. *The Leadership Quarterly*, *18*(5), 477–489. doi:10.1016/j.leaqua.2007.07.004

Wasti, S. A., Tan, H. H., Brower, H. H., & Önder, Ç. (2007). Cross-cultural measurement of supervisor trustworthiness: An assessment of measurement invariance across three cultures. *The Leadership Quarterly*, *18*(5), 477–489. doi:10.1016/j.leaqua.2007.07.004

Weiss, T., & Berger, R. (2006). Reliability and validity of a Spanish version of the Posttraumatic Growth Inventory. *Research on Social Work Practice*, *16*(2), 191–199. doi:10.1177/1049731505281374

Whisman, M. A., & Judd, C. M. (2016). A cross-national analysis of measurement invariance of the Satisfaction With Life Scale. *Psychological Assessment*, *28*(2), 239–244. doi:10.1037/pas0000181 PMID:26168309

Woods, C. M. (2009). Evaluation of MIMIC-model methods for DIF testing with comparison to two-groups analysis. *Multivariate Behavioral Research*, *44*(1), 1–27. doi:10.1080/00273170802620121 PMID:26795105

Wu, W., Lu, Y., Tan, F., Yao, S., Steca, P., Abela, J. Z., & Hankin, B. L. (2012). Assessing measurement invariance of the Childrens Depression Inventory in Chinese and Italian primary school student samples. *Assessment*, *19*(4), 506–516. doi:10.1177/1073191111421286 PMID:21911438

Xu, F., Hilpert, P., Randall, A. K., Li, Q., & Bodenmann, G. (2016). Validation of the Dyadic Coping Inventory with Chinese couples: Factorial structure, measurement invariance, and construct validity. *Psychological Assessment*, *28*(8), e127–e140. doi:10.1037/pas0000329 PMID:27183045

Yildirim, H. H., & Berberoglu, G. (2009). Judgmental and statistical DIF analyses of the pisa-2003 mathematics literacy items. *International Journal of Testing*, *9*(2), 108–121. doi:10.1080/15305050902880736

Yuan, K., & Chan, W. (2016). Measurement Invariance via Multigroup SEM: Issues and Solutions With Chi-Square-Difference Tests. *Psychological Methods*, *21*(3), 405–426. doi:10.1037/met0000080 PMID:27266799

Chapter 5

# Developing a Visual Assessment

## ABSTRACT

*Chapter 5 provides an example of an attempt to develop a visual assessment of extroversion. Two separate studies were conducted. In the first study, the complete process of image selection, evaluation, and validation of the instrument is provided. After the development of the instrument is complete, and illustration of how the cross-cultural equivalence was assessed across two cultures is provided. The second study extends the first study by including the text-based questions of the Big Five Inventory for both cultures, and by adding some simple text to the images. The chapter concludes with a discussion of steps that could be included to limit bias in such assessments.*

## INTRODUCTION

Can a visual assessment of personality be constructed that can be used across cultures? Or is the interpretation of images so bound to culture that it is impossible to find images that would be culturally neutral? Those are the questions being explored in this Chapter. An image-based assessment designed to measure the Big 5 personality traits (openness, conscientiousness, extroversion, agreeableness, neuroticism) is explored across two cultures: One Western culture, the US, and one Eastern culture, India. The structure of this chapter is as follows:

DOI: 10.4018/978-1-5225-2691-9.ch005

- A description of the Big 5 Personality measure
- A review of cross-cultural research on the traditional Big Five assessment
- A description of Study 1, that explains the process of constructing a visual assessment of extroversion, and an analysis of data from the two countries
- A description of Study 2, which extends Study 1, with the addition of text to the images
- A summary of the findings of the chapter

In this chapter, only one subscale will be presented, extroversion, to illustrate the process of designing, evaluating and validating such a measure. The same process would be undertaken for the remaining four subscales. Respondents would receive a score on all the dimensions of the scale; however, since the traits are not overlapping, they are typically measured separately. Since the primary interest of this illustration is discovering how well images generalize across cultures, and not personality measurement per se, for the sake of space, only one scale is fully developed and illustrated here. Data were collected across two cultures to compare how well the images generalized across the cultures. While it is likely that other cultures would also be interesting to test, the initial exploration is using only two cultures to investigate the feasibility of developing such an assessment. Data were collected from both respondents in the United States as well as India using Amazon mechanical Turk software. India was chosen as the second county to choose a country with a large population, increasing the chance of variability in the responses, and also that was culturally dissimilar to the United States. Since most of the research on cultural equivalence of visual communication involved both Western and Eastern cultures, a similar strategy was chosen here, since that is where most of the cultural differences are likely to manifest.

In this chapter, two separate studies are described that sought to investigate the cultural equivalence of a visual assessment. Image selection, data collection, and evaluation of the resulting instrument are illustrated for two cultural groups in different contexts. To better understand the process involved in constructing the instrument/assessment, it is helpful to understand something about the original assessment on which this visual assessment was based. Therefore, a description of the Big Five Inventory precedes the discussion of constructing the visual assessment.

# DESCRIPTION OF THE BIG FIVE INVENTORY

The Big Five Personality Inventory is one of the most widely used personality assessments (John & Srivastava, 2008). The inventory has an interesting history, in that it was not developed from an existing theory, but rather the theory was developed based on empirical data analysis of terms people use to describe themselves (John & Srivastava, 2008). Because of its unusual history, some background is provided, as it is relevant to the development of the visual assessment. As early as 1936, a group of psychologists extracted all of the personality-relevant terms from the unabridged English dictionary (John & Srivastava, 2008). Over 18,000 words were extracted, and for the next 60 years, psychologists attempted to create a taxonomy of personality using this list of 18,000 words. Allport and Odbert (1936) classified the original 18,000 terms into categories including personality, moods, personal conduct, and physical characteristics. In 1943 Catell used the subset of 4,500 terms in the personality category to use empirical data analysis techniques to try to reduce these terms into groups of terms that would represent personality traits, and was able to reduce the list of traits from 4,500 to 35 terms. Now that the list of terms was much more manageable, other psychologists began to investigate the construct of personality. Fiske (1949) used 22 of the terms of Catell's and had people report on their identification with the terms, as well as reports about the respondent from others. Analyzing these responses led to a factor structure that was very similar to what would become known as the Big Five. Tupes and Christal (1961) collected data from multiple groups of people and found five factors that recurred in all samples. The five-factor structure has been replicated by many other psychologists (Norman, 1963; Borgatta, 1964; Digman & Takemoto-Chock, 1981), and is widely accepted as the dominant theory of personality. The five traits were originally described as:

1. Extraversion or Surgency (talkative, assertive, energetic);
2. Agreeableness (good-natured, cooperative, trustworthy);
3. Conscientiousness (orderly, responsible, dependable);
4. Emotional Stability vs. Neuroticism (calm, not easily upset);
5. Culture (intellectual, polished, independent-minded) (John & Srivastava, 2008).

The modern version of the Big Five is not that different, and is often referred to as OCEAN:

1. Openness v. Practical
2. Conscientiousness v. Spontaneous
3. Extroversion v. Introversion
4. Agreeableness v. Independence
5. Neuroticism v. Emotional Stability

These five broad traits were associated with finer grain-sized traits. For example, openness was associated with curious, imaginative, artistic, wide interests, excitable and unconventional. Conscientiousness consists of competence, order, dutifulness, achievement striving, self-discipline and deliberation. Extroversion is associated with sociable, assertive, energetic, adventurous, enthusiastic and outgoing. Agreeableness is related to trusting, straightforward, warm, compliant, modest and sympathetic. And neuroticism is related to the traits of anxiety, irritability, depressed, self-conscious, impulsive and vulnerable. For each of these broad 5 categories, there are numerous traits that are identified with each broad category, making each of the five factors very multifaceted.

To measure these traits, there are variations of the instrument, but all of them are quite similar. Respondents are presented with a series of statements, and they rate the degree to which they agree with each statement. For example, an item might be "I see myself as someone who is talkative." The respondent rates this item as "Strongly Agree," "Somewhat Agree," "Neutral," "Somewhat Disagree," or "Strongly Disagree" (a list of the items on the instrument is provided in Appendix A).

## CROSS-CULTURAL RESEARCH ON BIG FIVE INVENTORY

Before embarking on creating a visual personality assessment that can be used cross-culturally, evidence that the construct is generalizable across cultures is necessary. There has been interest in research on the cross-cultural measurement of personality, and several articles have published the results of the validation of translations of the Big Five Inventory. Congruence between the English version and other language versions have been found for Spanish (Benet-Martinez & Oliver, 1998) Dutch (Denissen, Geenen, van Aken, Gosling, & Potter, 2008), Croatian (Mlacic & Glodberg, 2007), Italian (Ubbiali, Chiorri, Hampton, & Donati, 2013), as well as other languages. Schmitt, Allik, McCrae, and Benet-Martinez (2007) did a study of the Big

Five Inventory that included 56 nations and found support for the five-factor structure.

Clearly the interest is there for the creation of translated version of the inventory, and the inventory does appear to be work in multiple cultures. In addition to translations of the Big Five Inventory, a clearinghouse exists for people to submit items that they have translated from the International Personality Item Pool (IPIP). At this clearinghouse, there are 43 languages represented including Arabic, Bulgarian, Chinese, Croatian, Czech, Danish, Dutch, Estonia, Farsi, Finnish, French, German, Greek, Hebrew, Hungarian, Icelandic, Indonesian, Iranian, Italian, Japanese, Korean, Latvian, Lithuanian, Macedonian, Malay, Norwegian, Otjiherhero, Polish, Portuguese, Romanian, Russian, Serbian, Slovak, Slovene, Spanish, Mexican Spanish, Swedish, Thai, Turkish, Urdu, Vietnamese, and Welsh. Researchers who have translated the items can make them available for use, and for many languages, there are multiple researchers that have submitted translations. This repository is an indicator of the interest in using personality measures in research across cultures.

Interestingly, there is one study that was found that attempted to translate the Big Five Inventory to use with Chinese smokers (Leung, Wong, Chan, & Lam, 2012). Although this is a limited sample of Chinese people, and doesn't represent the entire population, this study represents the first study that has attempted to apply the instrument to an Eastern culture, rather than a Western culture. The results were interesting in that unlike in the European countries, the factor structure did not completely hold with the Chinese sample, and the instrument had to be modified for use. The full instrument was 44 items, and the modified instrument was 29 items. Of the 15 items that were deleted across the five factors, 12 were items that were to be reversed scored, or items that were measuring the opposite end of the spectrum, namely, introversion. This might indicate that there are issues with these types of items in this cultural context, as in the other languages this was not an issue. Attention should be paid to this issues moving forward in cross-cultural research. In the extraversion scale, only two items were deleted: "Is reserved", and "Has an assertive personality." The item "Is reserved" would be an example of the item that would be reversed scored, as it is the opposite of extraversion.

In addition to research on the full Big Five Inventory, there are shorter forms that have been developed to reduce the time it takes to administer and take the assessment. There has been much less research regarding the use of these brief instruments in other languages. Notable exceptions include German (Muck, Hell, & Gosling, 2007; Rammstedt & John 2007) and Swedish (Hochwalder, 2006). One popular brief instrument is the Big Five Mini Markers (Saucier, 1994). In this form of the assessment, instead of full sentences, the respondents are provided a list of adjectives, and they have to rate the extent to which that adjective describes them. In the original version of the assessment, the respondents use a nine point rating scale. This scale was examined for its use internationally, although in English. That is, Thompson validated it using a multinational population of both native and non-native English speakers in 2008. The nations included in the final study were Burma, China, Hungary, India, Indonesia, Japan, Malaysia, Philippines, Taiwan, Thailand, and Vietnam. Interestingly there are all non-European nations, which is where the problems are likely to exist across cultures. When used with non-native English speakers, the factor structure and reliability of the original instrument did not represent good psychometric properties. There were items that did not load on the intended factors, and had high cross-loadings. Additionally, reliabilities were lower than 0.70 (Thompson, 2008). The instrument was then revised using the multinational sample of data through several iterations. Items that were of poor quality were removed, and substituted with better functioning items. Poor quality items were items with low factor loadings or high cross loadings. These items were also reviewed qualitatively, and the items were identified as not familiar (bashful, bold, fretful, temperamental, withdrawn), colloquial (sloppy, touchy) or ambiguous in meaning across cultures (complex, relaxed). For the extraversion scale, the items bashful, bold, and withdrawn were not functioning well. Interestingly, two of the three items were items related to introversion, which were the types of items that were poorly functioning in the Chinese translation of the original Big Five Inventory. The final items in the scale were talkative, untalkative, quiet, outgoing, extroverted, shy, reserved, energetic, creative.

In addition to removing these items, and replacing them, the response scale was reduced from nine points to five points (1=Inaccurate, 5=Accurate), to make the instrument shorter.

The next section of this chapter presents two studies that were undertaken to attempt to construct a visual assessment of extraversion to be used in two different cultures.

## STUDY 1

The first study illustrates the steps in constructing a visual assessments and evaluating the cross-cultural equivalence of the resulting assessment.

A description of the image selection is provided, data collection methods, and final item selection. The image selection for the final assessment form was an iterative process, and all steps are outlined. For the final assessment form, the cultural equivalence of the form was assessed across a US sample and a sample from Hindi speaking India. This process was illustrated using the data gathered.

## Selecting Images

When developing the image-based assessment, the process of choosing the most appropriate images was not always clear or straightforward. Just as it was not easy to construct the original text-based instrument, it was not easy to construct the image-based version. Some of the difficulty arose because of the nature of the Big Five inventory. Since each of the Big Five Factors is multifaceted, it was not clear how to choose images to reflect the multifaceted nature of each of the larger traits. In addition, the Big Five inventory was not based on any theory of personality, but was the result of analyzing empirical data. In the same way, the construction of the visual assessment was also in part an empirical process, although there was the theory suggested by the Big Five Factors to guide the process. An iterative process was used where the data from the data collection was used to refine the choice of images. For illustration, only the discussion of creating the Extraversion scale is included here, although the same process was used across the other four factors. For the creation of the scale, only data from the United States sample was used to create and refine the assessment. To create the extroversion scale, the traits that are associated with extroversion: sociable, assertive, energetic, adventurous, enthusiastic and outgoing, were identified, and then used to identify images that would exemplify these traits. The traits of being adventurous, liking speed, and images that contain motion like rollercoasters or blurry pictures depicting movement might be appropriate for eliciting extroversion. Additionally, images depicting crowds, group events, or sports might be appealing. To include the opposite end of the spectrum, images that depicted introversion were also chosen, to be able to differentiate those who identified as introverts from those that identify as extroverts. Since the scale is extraversion, the traits associated with introversion are not explicitly stated, but can be assumed to be the opposite of the traits included in extroversion. For example, instead of sociable, introverts might like to be solitary, instead of assertive, they could be passive, instead of energetic, they could be calm, and instead of adventurous, they could be cautious. Images for introverts, therefore, might include images of being alone, reading, or doing solitary activities, or quiet places might be appealing. However, it is important to notice that there is some blurring between some of the traits, so it was important to be careful not to confuse being alone, with being lonely. In the case of being alone, or solitary, the introvert is happy to be alone, and would not be lonely. Therefore, when choosing an image of a person alone, it was important that the person did not seem lonely, but rather seemed to be happy to be alone, doing solitary activities, such as reading a book, or walking in the woods.

Once the traits and potential images were defined, the selection of images occurred. There are many different options for choosing images. The images could be photos or drawing, they could already exist in a library of images, or could be created for the purposes of the assessment. Each of these options has its advantages and disadvantages. We chose to use photographs rather than drawings based on the research around the potential for "factual" images to translate across cultures more easily than symbols. While drawing would not necessarily be symbols, photographs seemed to be more "realistic" and could depict events that might be familiar to people.

The choice between selecting pre-existing images and creating images is also not very obvious. Creating images for the specific purpose of the assessment would have provided a level of control that was not available in using pre-existing images. However, using pre-existing images allowed for a more practical solution. Pre-existing images were used for convenience and cost. Additionally, as this research is exploratory, expending the cost of creating images was deemed excessive. However, in subsequent iterations, using a set of images that are likely candidates can provide evidence as to how to compose the images for future assessments. In that case, control over all factors can be manipulated and modified to find the best set of images. This idea is discussed more fully in the future direction chapter of the book.

Using the definitions of the traits, an initial set of images was selected for use in the assessment using a public database (www.rf123.com). A set of 18 images was tested initially to attempt to define a subset of images that were best representing the construct of extraversion. For each image, respondents were asked to rate the image as "like me" or "not like me." These were the response options provided to the respondent, and the only text in the assessment, aside from the directions.

The research questions addressed in this study were:

1.  Can a visual assessment of personality that is text-free be developed that is reliable and valid?
2.  Can a visual assessment of personality be used across different cultures? Specifically, US and India?

## Initial Data Collection

Using the initial set of images selected, data were collected from people in the United States. A random group of respondents were collected using Amazon Mechanical Turk (mTurk), an online crowd sourcing software that has gained popularity as a relatively inexpensive, and fast way to collect data (Buhrmester, Kwang, & Gosling, 2011). Using this technology, the instrument was able to be administered, and collect the data fairly easily. Approximately 200 respondents were recruited. Respondents were paid a nominal fee for their time. This initial data collection served the goal of evaluating the initial set of items, to determine a set of images that could be administered to another country in subsequent data collections.

## Evaluating the Item Quality

Several analyses were conducted to evaluate the item quality. The first analyses were done to determine whether the image could differentiate among people. The assumption was that there would be both introverts and extraverts in the sample. For each item, the number of people who chose "like me" and "not like me" was computed. If, for example, all the respondents chose "like me" for an item, it would indicate that either the image did not differentiate very well among different types of people, or the sample of examinees were all introverts or all extraverts.

Once it was determined that the items showed some level of discrimination, or differentiation, the factor structure of the data was examined. This would follow the process used for constructing the original Big Five Inventory, where empirical data would be used to support the choice of items/images. It would be expected that introversion and extroversion be on opposite sides of one continuum. However, in the initial data collection, it appeared as though the images selected to measure extroversion were measuring a different trait than those selected to measure introversion, rather than different ends of a continuum. If they were representing different ends of the same continuum, for example, factor loadings for extroversion would be positive, while factor loadings, on the same factor, would be negative. Instead, the two types of images were loading on two separate factors, or dimensions. This finding is consistent with the study of the Big Five Inventory in Chinese (Leung, Wong, Chan, & Lam, 2012) and also the development of the International Big Five Mini Markers (Thompson, 2008), where the introversion items were problematic. Perhaps that dimension of extraversion – introversion is not the same across Western and Eastern cultures. Extraversion might look similar in different cultures, but what constitutes the opposite of introversion might vary across cultures. The fact that there were multiple dimensions being uncovered in the data was not surprising given that these five factors are broad and represents a set of traits, not just one trait. Because of this result, a deeper examination of the images was warranted to refine the image selection.

Using the empirical data as a guide, the images depicting introversion were re-examined. While images were chosen to depict people as alone, some of the images that were selected to depict introversion looked more depression, or loneliness, where the subjects in the images looked upset, despondent, and lonely, not just alone. New images were selected that showed individuals alone, but content, or enjoying relaxing activities.

Another factor that was revealed appeared to be related to sports. Since extroversion includes traits like energetic, many of the images related to extroversion were related to sports, and these images appeared to represent a different dimension. It may or may not have actually been a different dimension, but one of the sub dimensions of extroversion. However, because we did not know whether the respondents were interpreting the images as a type of extroversion or as whether or not the enjoyed sports, which is not a property that is exclusive to extroverts, those images were removed from the set of images to be used on the instrument. Additionally, many of the images related to extroversion were often crowd-based, or partying-oriented. Again, respondents might not have seen those images as representing outgoing behavior, but partying behavior, that is separate from extroversion.

Based on these observations, and possible misinterpretations of the images, new images were collected. In this new set of images, images of extroversion that did not rely on sports, or crowds were chosen. Some of the images still depicted crowds, but instead of showing the crowds in party-type situations, the crowds were more about spending time with friends, perhaps taking a selfie together, or just sitting outdoors. An attempt was made to eliminate the alternate interpretations of the images to the best of our ability, while still retaining the core traits of extraversion. Similarly, for the introversion images, we found images of people alone, but we were careful to select images where the people looked content or happy to be alone, rather than lonely or depressed. Figure 1 provides an example of an image depicting introversion, and Figure 2 provides an example of an image depicting extroversion.

The empirical data shed an interesting light on the how differently people were interpreting the images than we intended them to. It was clear evidence that the images contained meaning that was not intended, and this was in a single culture, where the interpretations would be more similar than in different cultures. This process was clearly very complex.

## Second Data Collection

Using this new set of 18 images, data were collected again on a new sample of approximately 200 American respondents using Amazon mTurk. Because the images changed, the same item quality analysis was conducted. Using the results of the factor analysis on this set of items, a subset of eight images was chosen that appeared to measure one dimension. While it is not necessarily the case that extroversion is unidimensional, given the multifaceted aspects of these five traits, to be consistent with the original work on the Big Five personality traits, we created a unidimensional subset of items that appeared to capture both aspects of introversion and extroversion. This new set of images appeared to elicit responses more as expected, with the introversion and extroversion images representing opposite sides of a continuum. This

*Figure 1.*

*Figure 2.*

was determined using Exploratory Factor Analysis, where the factor loadings for the extroversion images were positive, and negative for the introversion images, as anticipated. This set of images was used for the cross-cultural comparison, as we believed it to be the best set of images we had found to measure the trait in the US context.

## Final Data Collection

In the final data collection, data were collected India from a random group of respondents, again using Amazon mTurk. Approximately 200 respondents were recruited from India.

## Translation

Because the assessment was image-based, there was very little need for translation. The responses of "like me" and "not like me" had to be translated. Since there are multiple languages spoken in India, we had to make a choice of what language to use. We chose to use Hindi, as it is the language spoken by the majority of people. With the simplicity of the text that needed translation, the translation was very straightforward, and did not need adapting to the different culture.

While the assessment itself was not text-heavy, the directions for answering the assessment also had to be translated. A professional translator was hired to perform this service. Since the use of Mechanical Turk in India is high (Ipeirotis, 2010) we felt that most respondents would be familiar with the environment and would be able to navigate the survey with little prompting anyway. However, we did translate all instructions.

## Validation

In addition to comparing the responses to the images across the two cultures it was important to ascertain that the assessment was actually measuring what it was intended to measure, namely, extroversion. To determine this, the traditional text-based introversion/extroversion subscale of the Big Five personality measure (Costa & McCrae, 1985) was also administered to the sample in the United States, where translation would not be an issue. Using the responses to both the images and the text-based questions it was possible e to determine the extent to which these two measures measure the same thing. Since the text-based assessment has already been validated, if the image-based measure correlates with the text-based measure, then there would be evidence that the two instruments were measuring the same underlying construct. To that end, for the United States sample, the score on the text-based questions and the image-based questions correlated at 0.61. This level of correlation is the same as those observed with the VisualDNA versions of the visual assessments of personality (Visual DNA, 2016). This correlation is suggestive of strong convergent validity evidence between the visual assessment and the text-based counterpart (Chamorro-Premuzic & Ahmetoglu, 2013).

One issue in creating the correlation between these two measures is a restricted range of the image-based assessment as compared to the text-based assessment. The image-based assessment offers only two response options: "Like Me" and "Not Like Me." This offers less room for variability in the total score of the responses. In contrast, the text-based questions allow for 5 different categories of responses: Strongly Agree, Somewhat Agree, Neutral, Somewhat Disagree, and Strongly Disagree. Due to the fact that there are more response options, the score range for the total score on the text-based assessment is 8-40, while the score range on the image-based version is only 8-16. This restricted range on the image-based assessment can artificially decrease the magnitude of the correlation coefficient.

## Item Analysis

The item analysis was then performed on the new US sample, as well as the Hindi speaking India sample (from here on referred to as the Hindi sample). As before, the first check was to ensure that for each item, there were people who selected both "like me" and "not like me" to ensure that there was variability in both samples. Again, if, for example, all the respondents chose "like me" for an item, it would indicate that the image did not differentiate very well among different people, or that the sample of people were all introverts or extroverts. It seemed unlikely that there were not both types of respondents in the sample, so items that did not have responses in both categories would be eliminated.

The proportion of people choosing each option was compared across the two samples (US and Hindi). These results are presented in Table 1. It was not necessarily expected that the proportion of people choosing each option would be similar across the two cultures, since there is no reason that extroversion would be equally prevalent in the two samples, although the national rates of extraversion are similar in US and India (Lynn & Martin, 1995). As such, differences between the groups are not an indicator that the construct varies across the cultures, just that the prevalence of the trait might vary across the samples. As seen in Table 1, all items in the assessment had people endorsing the item in each culture. In the US sample, there was a more dramatic split in the sample in terms of the percent of respondents endorsing or not endorsing the item, as opposed to the Hindi sample, where there was more of an even distribution of responses across the "Like Me" and "Not Like Me" categories.

*Table 1. Percent of respondents endorsing the image as "like me" for each culture*

| Image Number | US Sample | Hindi Sample |
|---|---|---|
| 1 | 30.5 | 53.3 |
| 2 | 22.5 | 53.8 |
| 3 | 26.0 | 66.0 |
| 4 | 47.5 | 63.0 |
| 5 | 33.5 | 60.5 |
| 6 | 31.5 | 62.5 |
| 7 | 62.7 | 67.5 |
| 8 | 44.0 | 76.5 |

These discrepancies would point that there are differences in the percent of respondents who identify as extroverted in each sample.

To determine the ability of each image to differentiate introverts and extroverts, the corrected item-total correlation was compute for each image. That quantity is the correlation between the response to the image and the total score, excluding the score on the one image in the computation of the total score (to reduce the bias in the correlation). Ideally, for a sound instrument, there should be a moderate correlation between the item score and the total score on the assessment. The items with higher correlations would be of higher quality, and items with very low correlation would likely not be as closely related to the construct of interest. These correlations were computed for the US and Hindi samples, and in this case, it would be expected that there would be similarities between the two groups of respondents. Table 2 presents the correlations for each image in both cultural groups. For some of the images, the differences in the correlation were large (image 1, image 5, image 8), however for the remaining five images the correlations are quite similar, indicating that a subset of items appears to be functioning similarly in the two samples.

## Dimensionality

Since the images were chosen to represent a single dimension based on a different sample of the US data, it would be expected that the instrument was still unidimensional in the US sample. However, since the items were chosen using the US sample, it was not clear what the dimensionality would be in the Hindi sample. To investigate the dimensionality, an exploratory factor analysis was conducted on the two samples of data. Table 3 provides the

*Table 2. Corrected item: total correlations of each item by sample*

| Image Number | US Sample | Hindi Sample |
| --- | --- | --- |
| 1 | 0.32 | 0.14 |
| 2 | 0.38 | 0.26 |
| 3 | 0.35 | 0.30 |
| 4 | 0.54 | 0.50 |
| 5 | 0.47 | 0.29 |
| 6 | 0.37 | 0.45 |
| 7 | 0.27 | 0.37 |
| 8 | 0.52 | 0.30 |

*Table 3. Total variance explained for first two factors: US and Hindi samples*

| Factor | Sample | Eigenvalue | Variance Explained |
|--------|--------|------------|--------------------|
| 1 | US | 2.70 | 33.79 |
| | Hindi | 1.95 | 38.94 |
| 2 | US | 0.98 | 12.23 |
| | Hindi | 0.92 | 18.31 |

results of the factor analysis for both samples. One criterion used to determine how many factors underlie a data set is the magnitude of the eigenvalues. A common criterion is to acknowledge factors with eigenvalues greater than 1. In addition, the difference in the magnitude of the first two eigenvalues can be used as evidence of unidimensionality. That is, if the first eigenvalue is substantially larger than the second, then there is evidence that the data are unidimensional. Given the large eigenvalues for the first factor, and the relatively small eigenvalues for the second factor, the instrument was determined to be unidimensional in both the US and Hindi samples.

In addition to both data sets exhibiting unidimensionality, the percent of variance explained by the first factor is similar across the two data sets, which is an indication that there might be a similar structure to the data.

## Reliability

Since the instrument was determined to be unidimensional, finding the reliability of the sample using coefficient alpha was appropriate. Coefficient alpha represents the degree of internal consistency among the items on the instrument. The reliability was determined to be 0.71 for the US sample and 0.63 for Hindi sample, as indicated in Table 4. The standard for acceptable reliability is approximately 0.70, although higher is better. It is important to remember, however, that these items represent only a subscale of the larger personality assessment. Therefore, the reliability of the subtest can be a bit less than would be expected for the full battery. The reliability in the US sample would be considered sufficient for a full assessment, and quite strong for a subscale measure. In the Hindi sample, while the reliability is somewhat lower, it would be marginal for a complete scale and appropriate for a subscale. While the reliability in the US sample is higher than in the Hindi sample, the difference was not too dramatic.

*Table 4. Reliability of measure by culture*

| Sample | Reliability |
|---|---|
| United States | 0.71 |
| Hindi | 0.63 |

## Equivalence of Items: Measurement Invariance

Once the scale was determined to be functioning reasonably in each of the two groups separately, the equivalence of the items could be assessed between the two groups. It is through these analyses that we can investigate the cross-cultural equivalence of the items. Recall that the primary reason to establish the equivalence of the items across cultures is so that the instrument can be used in different cultures, and the resulting scores would have the same meaning.

As discussed in Chapter 4, one analysis that can be conducted to determine the equivalence of the measures is to look at the measurement invariance of the items across groups. A specific type of measurement invariance can be classified as Differential Item Functioning, or DIF. In DIF analyses, respondents are matched on the trait of interest, in our example, level of extroversion, and then the probability of endorsing an image as "Like Me" is compared for the two groups. The idea is that people with the same level of extroversion should endorse the image with similar frequency, regardless of culture. However, if the two cultures have different frequencies of endorsement (i.e., probability of endorsement), after matching on level of extroversion, then that item would be flagged as exhibiting DIF. It is important to note that items can be flagged as exhibiting DIF even in the case that there is no true difference between the probabilities in the two groups. This can happen when random chance occurs, and the flagging is the result of error. This error is not a mistake in applying the detection method, but rather an error in the computation of the probability of endorsement due to random sampling error in the data.

When conducting DIF analyses, one key component to the design is the choice of what to use as a matching variable. Typically, in these analyses the score on the instrument itself is used as the matching criterion. When using this as a matching variable, there are two options for how to measure that score. In one case, the observed total score (sum of the points on the instrument) on the assessment can be used to designate the level of extroversion. The other option is to use an estimate of a latent trait of extroversion as the matching variable. This approach is usually favored, as the estimation of a latent trait would result in removing measurement error from the matching variable, making the matching more accurate. To this end, a latent variable approach was chosen.

Typically when a latent variable design is used, it is usually in the form of Structural Equation Modeling. The options include using a multiple-indicators multiple-causes (MIMIC) model, also referred to as Confirmatory Factor Analysis with Covariates, or a multiple group analysis. There are advantages and disadvantages to both models. The MIMIC model is more parsimonious, meaning that fewer parameters need to be estimated, making this model attractive when sample sizes are smaller. The downside to the MIMIC model is that it does not allow for the full testing of all the levels of measurement invariance that the multiple group analysis would allow for, and that were discussed in Chapter 3. Given the sample size used in this study, the MIMIC model was chosen. This approach has been determined to have adequate power, and controlled Type I error rate, even with small samples (Rick & Monroe, 2016). The details of the MIMIC model used in the analysis are provided.

To perform the analysis, first a model is chosen that specifies that factor structure of the assessment. As noted above, an exploratory factor analysis indicated that the instrument was unidimensional for each of the cultures. In each sample, the one-dimensional solution explained approximately 35% of the variability, with a clear dominant first factor. The first step in the process is to be sure that the confirmatory factor analysis model also indicates good fit. The CFA indicated that the instrument was indeed unidimensional in both samples, with model fit indices all in acceptable range. Since the unidimensional model was shown to fit, the model was specified as indicated in Figure 3.

This model indicates that the eight images are all indicators of the single latent variable, extroversion, denoted $n$, with the covariate of country. In this baseline model, the effect of country on the responses is indirect, as its influence on the responses is exhibited only through the latent variable. Once this model was shown to display adequate fit, the direct effect of the country on the item responses, as shown in Figure 4.

In this case, the dotted arrow between the covariate, country, is pointing directly to the image 8, indicating that the response to image 8 is *directly* effected by country membership, and this effect is *separate* than the effect of the latent variable (extroversion) on the response. If this effect is significant, then the implication that there is something in the covariate that is not extroversion that is influencing the response to the images. In this instance, the item is said to exhibit DIF. This figure demonstrates the model for testing to determine

*Figure 3.*

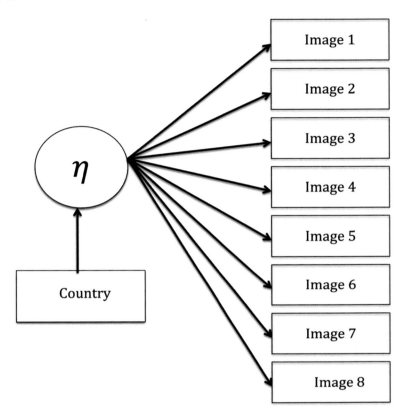

if item eight exhibits DIF, as testing for the significance of that direct effect is testing for DIF. The same model was tested for each item individually; to determine in which items the direct effect of country on item response was significant, indicating DIF. This analysis indicated that there were three items that were flagged as exhibiting DIF. These items were images 1, 5, and 7.

Once the items that exhibited DIF were identified, these items were examined to determine if there was a clear reason why those particular items were flagged, while others were not. An example of an item exhibiting DIF is presented in Figure 4, which was intended to indicate extroversion. In this image, a woman is pointing up with her index fingers extended and looks excited. This image might have several issues, when the criteria laid forth in Chapter 2 are considered. First, while some might interpret her expression as happy, it is not unambiguous what emotion her expression is showing. Given that she is wearing a red shirt, the interpretation might vary across cultures,

*Figure 4.*

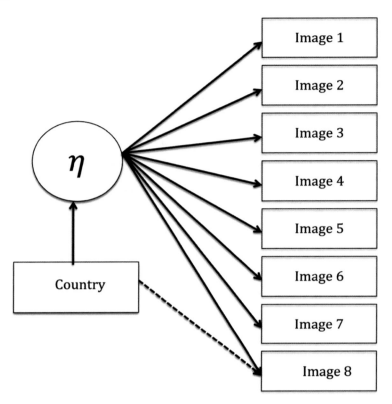

as red is a color that has different meanings, especially across Eastern and Western cultures. Lastly, as indicated previously in Chapter 2, hand gestures have different meanings in different cultures, and one theory to explore is that this image has meaning that varies to the two different cultures. This could be verified by interviewing respondents on what the images mean to them. On the positive side, the image is clean in that it does not have any background images that might confuse the respondent as to what part of the image is the intended focus.

Figure 6, in contrast, depicts and image that was not flagged as exhibiting DIF across the two cultures. This image was also chosen to depict extroversion, and shows a group of people at a concert. This image does not clearly show the faces of the people in the crowd, and does not have very distinct colors present. Also, there is not a lot of background imagery to distract from the focus of the image. All of these characteristics might have lead to its culturally neutral tone.

*Figure 5.*

*Figure 6.*

Of the eight images used in this subscale, five of the eight showed no indication of DIF, meaning that the responses that people gave to the images were based on their level of the latent trait, extroversion, and not on the culture to which the respondent belongs. This result provides promise for building assessments using images that can be used in multiple cultures, alleviating the need for translation. While a large number of images might need to be tested to identify those that are culturally neutral, the same is true for developing text-based items. The job here is actually easier, since no costly translations need to be undertaken to create items that might *potentially* be useful.

To create an instrument that could be reliably used across cultures, then, the five items that did not exhibit DIF could be used as a measure of extroversion that was invariant across the two cultures. By shortening the scale to five items, however, the reliability of the measure would change. The Hindi sample reliability was reduced to 0.60 (0.63 with 8 items), and the US reliability was reduced to 0.66 (0.73 with 8 items). While these reliabilities are probably still reasonable for a subtest, they are reduced a bit from the original reliabilities. Selecting better images to replace the ones that were removed for exhibiting DIF could increase the reliability of the subtest.

## Research Questions

The above analyses provided data to answer the research questions put forth in this study. This section summarizes the results of the analyses related to each of the research questions, and provides a response.

- The first research question was, "Can a visual assessment of personality that is text-free be developed that is reliable and valid?" There is evidence presented here that there is evidence of convergent validity through the correlation of the scores on the image-based assessment and the text-based assessment. Given the reasonable level of reliability as well, and the pilot nature of the study, the evidence presented here is convincing that it would be possible to build an even better assessment that is text-free.
- The second research question asked, "Can a visual assessment of personality be used across different cultures? Specifically, US and India?" This answer is also yes. While it was not easy to necessarily find those images, it was possible to find images that did not exhibit DIF across the two cultures. This provides evidence that it is possible

to find images that can transcend these two cultures. Including more cultures increases the complexity, but there is reason to believe it is possible.

## Strategies for Reducing Bias

Two taxonomies were presented in the book that can be used to help understand how bias might be reduced. There was the taxonomy in Chapter 2, which provided the features of the images that might lead to culturally sensitive images. The DIF items were evaluated in the text above relative to this taxonomy. In the 3 DIF items, there were several violations of the taxonomy. In two of the items (Items 5 and 7), the person in the image was wearing red. In one of the images (item 5), the person in the image was also using hand gestures. Item 1, which was also identified as exhibiting DIF was an image showing the back of the heads of a large group of people at a concert, or some event. It is not clear why this item exhibited DIF when evaluated using the taxonomy from Chapter 2. These results provide some validity to the taxonomy as presented by Bresciani and Epell (2010b).

The second taxonomy was presented in Chapter 3, which was a taxonomy of the types of bias that exist in cross-cultural assessments and strategies for handling that type of bias. The three types of bias were construct, method and item bias. For construct bias, six strategies were provided to handle this type of bias. In this study, only 2 of the six strategies were employed: (1) use sample of examinees across multiple cultures and (2) develop the measures in the separate cultures and then administer them across multiple cultures. Including the other strategies, where possible might have led to a greater number of images that were invariant across the two cultures.

For method bias, one of the three strategies was employed: assessment of the response styles of respondents. In this case, the sample from India was chosen for the very reason that a large percentage of users of mTurk lived in India, so the interface would be familiar. This type of bias was not likely to be very problematic in this study, since familiar tools were used in both cultures to gather the data.

Lastly, item bias was addressed using one of the three strategies: differential item functioning/measurement invariance. Like the construct bias, employing other strategies to address item bias, specifically, the judgmental review of items by experts in both cultures would likely have led to a greater number of items that were invariant across cultures.

## Explanation of DIF

The taxonomy in Chapter 2 regarding the features of items that might be sensitive across cultures can potentially help explain why the DIF was observed. In the 3 DIF items, there were several violations of the taxonomy. In two of the items (Items 5 and 7), the person in the image was wearing red. In one of the images (item 5), the person in the image was also using hand gestures. Item 1, which was also identified as exhibiting DIF was an image showing the back of the heads of a large group of people at a concert, or some event. It is not clear why this item exhibited DIF when evaluated using this taxonomy. These results do provide some validity to the taxonomy as presented by Bresciani and Eppler (2010b).

## STUDY 2

The second study was an extension of the first study. In the second study, 16 of the original 17 images were used that were used as in the initial data collection in the first study. One image was deleted after viewing the item in the context of this study, and realizing it didn't fit the study well. In this study, however, in addition to the images, text was added along with the images, to guide the focus of the respondent. As noted in the taxonomy in Chapter 2 regarding how different cultures interpret images, culture influences what the focus of the image is, and also how the image is interpreted. By adding some minor language, in addition to the image, the goal is to guide the focus of the respondent to what the image is intended to display. The text was kept as simple as possible, to minimize the translation burden of the assessment, as one of the goals is to minimize, or preferably, eliminate text from the assessment process. In making this modification, insight will be gained into whether it is the interpretation of the image that is leading to the differences in the responses, or if it is something different. This format is more similar to that used by Traitify (2016) in their image-based personality assessments. The type of text that was added to the image was text like, "I like large crowds" or "I enjoy being alone." The text was generated and reviewed by three psychologists.

The choice of text to add to the images was not as simple as it might sound. Because the text was to be as simple as possible, it was necessary to make it clear and precise in what was trying to be conveyed to the respondent. To facilitate this process, a grid of attributes related to extraversion was created with adjectives that described both ends of the spectrum as well as the more moderate levels of introversion or extraversion. This grid is reproduced in Table 5.

This grid aided in the development of the text to be used on the images. Text included with the images include the following words or phrases:

- Reserved
- Socially Reserved
- Enjoys Time Alone
- Enthusiastic
- Full of Energy
- Low-key
- Works Alone
- Action Oriented
- Cautious
- Restored by Solitude
- Recharged by Others
- Reflective
- Enjoys Crowds
- Center of Attention
- Enjoy Big Parties
- Part of Crowd

*Table 5. General descriptions for levels of extraversion*

| EXTRAVERT: General Description | Extraversion is characterized by: breadth rather than depth of activities, energy gained from external activity/situations rather than internal, enjoyment in interaction with others, full of energy, enthusiastic, action-oriented, enjoy talking, being visible, assertive. |
|---|---|
| High Scoring | You are an extravert. You are outgoing, talkative, and you enjoy being around people. You are very enthusiastic with lots of energy, and at times a bit assertive. You need lots of stimulation so you are not bored. You are energized by being around other people. |
| Medium | You are sometimes an introvert, and sometimes an extravert. So long as you are comfortable with the people around you - you will tend towards extraversion, but with a group of less familiar people you may be more quiet and reluctant to be social. Although sometime nervous in social situations, you are deliberate in making long-term friendships. |
| Low | You are an introvert. You don't want to be the center of attention, and alone time helps you to recharge. You tend to be quiet and very deliberate. You are also very creative and enjoy learning new thing things. |
| INTROVERT: General Description | Introverts are characterized by: lower social engagement, lower energy, quiet, low-key, deliberate, independent of social world, as opposed to shy, needing less stimulation, need more alone time, reserved in social situations |

These words/phrases were generated based on the descriptions in the grid shown in Table 5. Therefore, it was anticipated to capture the aspects of the personality measure that the images were targeting.

The text-based questions from the Big Five Inventory were also included in this study. In the first study, the text-based questions were used only for the US sample, for validating the image-based assessment; in this study, the text-based questions were presented in both the US-based assessment and the India-based assessment. The text-based questions were translated to Hindi, as was the text on the image. After receiving feedback from one respondent regarding the ubiquity of English in India, the English version was also administered to a different sample in India, to eliminate any issues due to translation. The process of translation might result in an assessment that is less generalizable across cultures than the all-English version was. Because the assessment was offered in both Hindi and English, the terminology of Study 1 is modified. Instead of referring to the Hindi sample, we will refer to the India sample, and specify if it is the Hindi version or the English version.

The research questions explored in this study were:

1.  Does the addition of text enhance the factor structure of the data in both US and Indian samples? For the Indian sample, that includes bot the Hindi and English version of the assessment.
2.  Do scores on the text-based questions of the Big Five Inventory correlate with the data obtained from the visual assessment? This is a validation check of the visual assessment. Unlike Study 1, the validation will be done for both cultures, rather than for just the US sample.
3.  Are the images, with the addition of text, generalizable across the cultures?

## Data Collection

In this study, the data were only collected once from each group of respondents. First, data were obtained from the US sample and the India sample using the translated version of the assessment. Based on feedback from respondents, due to the many languages spoken in India, English is often used as a common language. As such, in addition to the planned two samples, a third sample was included in a second data collection. In this case, the English version of the assessment was administered in India. The results presented here represent the data from the three samples: US, India-Hindi and India-English. This notation will be used going forward.

As noted before, all but one image of the original set of 17 images administered in the initial data collection of Study 1 were used for this study, not only the eight images that were ultimately selected in Study 1. Because the addition of text might make the focus of the image clearer, all images were included for the data collection process. Data were again collected from people in the United States and India. A random group of respondents were collected using Amazon Mechanical Turk (mTurk). Approximately 200 respondents were recruited from each country. In this initial data collection, only the Hindi version of the assessment was administered in India. Respondents were paid a nominal fee for their time.

## Evaluating Item Quality

As with the first study, the task was to evaluate the item quality. Since the format of the items changed between studies, this step was necessary to repeat. First the frequencies of the responses of "like me" and "not like me" were tabulated for both versions of the assessment. Again, there is no reason to believe they would be similar across the two cultures, it was important to ensure that there were respondents that identified with each category. For each of the three samples, the number of respondents that chose "like me" is presented in Table 6.

When comparing across the samples, the two Indian samples performed similarly, whether the assessment was administered in Hindi or English, providing some evidence of the comparability of the two forms. When comparing the Indian and US samples, however, there are striking differences, where clearly there are more people that would be identified as extroverts in the Indian sample than in the US sample, as indicated by the much smaller percent of people choosing the "like me" option. Since images that depicted introversion were reverse-coded so that they would be scored in the same direction as the other items, it appears that the US sample was predominantly introverted (as measured by this scale) and the Indian samples were predominantly extraverted (as measured by this scale).

When considering item quality, two items stand out in the US sample from this analysis. Images 6 and 15 have very small percentage of respondents choosing "like me" in the US sample. These very small samples might make these items less stable and are dropped from future analyses that include the US sample.

*Table 6. Percent of respondents endorsing the image as "like me" for each sample*

| Image Number | US | India-Hindi | India-English |
|:---:|:---:|:---:|:---:|
| 1 | 23.3 | 59.2 | 64.3 |
| 2 | 17.6 | 64.9 | 65.7 |
| 3 | 34.3 | 56.4 | 64.3 |
| 4 | 39.0 | 56.4 | 67.6 |
| 5 | 33.3 | 74.9 | 81.9 |
| 6 | 7.6 | 31.8 | 21.3 |
| 7 | 11.4 | 25.6 | 35.7 |
| 8 | 39.5 | 57.3 | 72.5 |
| 9 | 21.9 | 48.8 | 44.4 |
| 10 | 12.9 | 50.7 | 38.6 |
| 11 | 35.7 | 72.5 | 75.4 |
| 12 | 12.9 | 34.6 | 21.7 |
| 13 | 28.6 | 65.9 | 59.4 |
| 14 | 31.4 | 68.7 | 60.9 |
| 15 | 8.1 | 26.1 | 25.6 |
| 16 | 53.8 | 83.4 | 88.9 |

## Dimensionality

The dimensionality of the text-based questions was examined for each sample first. The US sample was clearly unidimensional, with a very large first eigenvalue (5.23) and 65 percent of the variability explained by the first factor. The first three eignevalues are provided in Table 7, where the first eigenvalue is clearly much larger than the second and third eigenvalues. This result is expected since the instrument was designed to be unidimensional for the subscale of extraversion. In both Indian samples, however, the scale was two-dimensional. The first three eigenvalues, and percent of variance explained by each factor are presented in Table 7. When the dimensions were examined, it appears that the items that measure introversion and the items that measure extraversion are on separate dimensions, unlike in the US sample. This result is consistent with what was found with the images in the first study, with introversion and extraversion loading on separate dimensions.

When examining the dimensionality of the image-based assessment, the initial set of 16 items was multidimensional in all three samples. For the US sample, the goal was to obtain a set of images depicting introversion and

*Table 7. Total variance explained for first two factors: US and Indian samples*

| Sample | Factor | Eigenvalue | Variance Explained |
|---|---|---|---|
| US | 1 | 5.23 | 65.42 |
| | 2 | 0.91 | 11.26 |
| | 3 | 0.64 | 8.02 |
| India-Hindi | 1 | 2.64 | 33.04 |
| | 2 | 1.83 | 22.82 |
| | 3 | 0.80 | 10.00 |
| India-English | 1 | 3.18 | 39.77 |
| | 2 | 1.55 | 19.41 |
| | 3 | 0.88 | 11.04 |

extraversion that was unidimensional, like the text-based version. Ten images were selected to represent that unidimensional construct, and include images chosen to depict introversion as well as extraversion. Five of the eight items selected for the final scale in Study 1 were selected for this set of images. These ten items include six images related to extraversion and four items related to introversion.

When the factor analysis was conducted using the Indian samples, the factor analysis revealed that the images associated with introversion and the items associated with extraversion loaded on different factors. As a result, these two sets of items were examined separately in these two samples. A subset of the introversion items and a subset of the extraversion items were found to be unidimensional in both samples. There were three items associated with extraversion, of the original six, and all four of the original items associated with introversion were retained.

The discrepancies across the samples indicate the difficulty in finding images that were common across the three samples. To understand more about why, the content of the images from the 10 items retained in the US sample was examined. It appeared that items related to energy levels "energetic," "low-key," and "action" formed a separate dimension in the Indian samples, but did not in the US sample. There might be something about the interaction between the level of energy required and the association with introversion and extraversion. In the US, the energy levels aligned with the trait: more energy was equated with extraversion where that was not observed in the Indian samples. This might be similar to what was observed in Study 1, where sport images were used. The resulting variability explained for the introversion and extraversion item sets, separately, for each sample, is provided in Table 8.

*Table 8. Total variance explained for first two factors: US and Indian samples*

| Sample | Factor | Eigenvalue | Variance Explained |
|---|---|---|---|
| US | 1: Introversion | 2.12 | 53.07 |
| | 2: Extraversion | 1.90 | 50.63 |
| India-Hindi | 1: Introversion | 1.47 | 35.75 |
| | 2: Extraversion | 1.19 | 39.49 |
| India-English | 1: Introversion | 1.57 | 39.25 |
| | 2: Extraversion | 1.42 | 42.37 |

It is clear that the assessment is measuring both sub-traits more strongly in the US sample as compared to either of the Indian samples, which are very similar to one another. This is made evident both by the larger percent of variance explained and the larger eigenvalues. The largest the eigenvalue could be, theoretically, is three, so closer to three is a stronger eigenvalue.

After the factor analysis, the final scale resulted in seven images. These seven images will be the basis for the analyses going forward.

## Item-Total Correlations

As with Study 1, once the final images were selected, the item-total correlations were computed to investigate the quality of the items. These correlations should be moderate to indicate good quality items. The correlations for each sample are presented in Table 9, and consistent with the results in other areas, the results are stronger for the US sample than for either of the Indian samples.

*Table 9. Corrected item: total correlations of each item by sample*

| Image Number | US | India-Hindi | India-English |
|---|---|---|---|
| 1 | .55 | .24 | .26 |
| 2 | .60 | .05 | .31 |
| 3 | .59 | .08 | .25 |
| 4 | .45 | .16 | .22 |
| 5 | .46 | .21 | .19 |
| 6 | .66 | .28 | .42 |
| 7 | .58 | .18 | .27 |

All of the items had strong correlations in the US sample, which is not surprising since the scale was very robust in the US sample. In the Indian-Hindi sample, there are two items that are of very low quality: image 2, and image 3, which have very low item-total correlations. Interestingly, in the India-English sample, the items look relatively good, although the correlations could be stronger; there are none that are very weak. The difference between the results of these two Indian samples is likely to the translation problem in translating the text between English and Hindi, since that was the only difference between these two conditions. If that result is true, it is an indication that having to translate text, even simple text, can be problematic, and lead to differences across cultures. Therefore, using images only might be more effective, even if there are differences in focus in the respondents.

## Reliability

The reliability of the resulting scales was also assessed across the three samples, and is presented in Table 10. Just as in Study 1, the reliability was assessed using coefficient alpha. The coefficient alpha is a measure of internal consistency, so it would be predicted to be lower in the Indian samples, where the images were not as strongly related to one another. The reliability of the US sample was quite good, at 0.81, but the reliability of the Indian sample were decidedly lower, at 0.39 for the India-Hindi sample, and 0.54 for the India-English sample. These reliabilities were lower for the Indian sample than the results in Study 1, where the reliability for the India-Hindi sample was 0.63. In that instance, adding the text to the images did not enhance the reliability of the assessment, and in fact, made it quite worse. When the Indian-English sample is considered, although the reliability is lower than the image-only assessment, it was much closer, indicating that translation issues might be the cause of the relatively poor performance in the Indian-Hindi sample. There was an improvement in the reliability of the US version of the

*Table 10. Reliability of measure by sample*

| Sample | Reliability |
|---|---|
| United States | 0.81 |
| India-Hindi | 0.39 |
| India-English | 0.54 |

assessment, with reliability increasing from 0.71 in the image-only version and 0.81 in the version with added text. Given this increase in reliability, similar improvements might be found in the Indian sample if a better translation were available, as would be likely in an assessment that was not a pilot test.

## Validation

The validation of the scales included computing the correlation between the scores of the image-based assessment and the text-based assessment. A higher correlation indicates greater agreement between the two measures. The correlations were done for the final seven-image form, as well as for the entire measure. In Study 1, this analysis was only performed for the US sample. The correlation in the US sample increased from Study 1; in Study 1, the correlation was 0.61, and in this Study, the correlation was 0.84 for the seven-image form and 0.86 for the total form. This represents a substantial improvement in how similar the two measures are. In the Indian samples, the correlations were much lower, with the India-Hindi sample having correlations of 0.33 for the seven-item form and 0.44 for the total form, and in the India-English sample, the correlations were stronger, at 0.56 for the seven-image form and 0.67 for the total form. These correlations are not very persuasive for the Indian versions of the form, although they indicate that the US version is quite strong with the introduction of the text.

## Item Bias Across Cultures

To assess the item bias, the same methodology used in Study 1, the MIMIC model, was used in this study, and hence will not be described again here. For each of the seven items, the influence of country on the performance of the item was assessed. In this case, country actually refers to sample: US, India-Hindi, India-English. The items that were flagged for DIF in the analysis were items 1, 2 and 6. An examination of the items does not make it clear why these items would exhibit DIF. For example, the image in Figure 7 was an example of an image that did exhibit DIF while the image in Figure 8 did not exhibit DIF. Given the similarities between these two items, it is surprising that one did exhibit DIF while the other one did not. Perhaps the issue was not with the image, but something with the text that was included with the image that caused the DIF.

*Figure 7.*

*Figure 8.*

## Strategies for Reducing Bias

Two taxonomies were presented in the book that can be used to help understand how bias might be reduced. There was the taxonomy in Chapter 2, which provided the features of the images that might lead to culturally sensitive images. The DIF items in this study did not appear to violate the features listed in this taxonomy. In the 3 DIF items, one of the items was flagged as exhibiting DIF in both studies. This is the image in Figure 9.

It is not clear why this item exhibited DIF when evaluated using the taxonomy from Chapter 2. Since it was flagged as DIF in both studies, there is something about this image that does not translate across these two cultures.

With respect to construct, method and item bias, similar to the first study, only two of the six strategies for construct bias were employed: (1) use sample of examinees across multiple cultures and (2) develop the measures in the separate cultures and then administer them across multiple cultures. Again, had other strategies been employed, there may have been a larger number of items that were invariant across the two cultures.

Just as in Study 1, method bias was addressed by choosing a response format that was familiar to the respondents. Only those familiar with mTurk would know to use mTurk. The format of this assessment would be familiar with most people who use the internet, as it was based on the style of popular

*Figure 9.*

internet quizzes. Item bias was assessed using a latent variable DIF detection method. Again, judgmental review would likely be helpful in choosing items that were more likely to be invariant across the cultures.

## Research Questions

The above analyses provided data to answer the research questions put forth in this study. This section summarizes the results of the analyses related to each of the research questions, and provides a response.

- The first research question was "Does the addition of text enhance the factor structure of the data in both US and Indian samples?" For the Indian samples, the answer is not clear. It was not possible to find a unidimensional solution with images depicting both introversion and extraversion in Study 2. The fact that there was a unidimensional solution in Study 1 does not mean that the solution actually depicted both aspects of extraversion. It is more likely that the interpretation of the images chosen to represent introversion were not interpreted to indicate introversion. This conclusion is supported by the analysis of the text-based questions, where introversion and extraversion items loaded on separate factors. Therefore, it could mean that this version of the assessment did a better job of uncovering the true factor structure than the image-only version did. For the US sample, it is clearer. Both Study 1 and Study 2 found a unidimensional solution, and in the Study 2 version, introversion and extraversion were more clearly represented, and the variance explained was higher in Study 2. Hence, it is fair to conclude that the version presented in Study 2 was a better representation of the expected factor structure.
- The second question asked, "Do scores on the text-based questions of the Big Five Inventory correlate with the data obtained from the visual assessment?" In Study 2, it was possible to assess this for all three versions of the assessment, unlike Study 1, where this was done only for the US sample. For the US sample, the correlation between the text-based questions and the image-based questions was quite high, 0.84, as opposed to 0.61 from Study 1. This is good evidence for convergent validity. For the India-Hindi sample the correlation was weak, 0.33 for seven images 0.44 if all the items were used. This is not very strong

evidence that the two instruments are measuring the same construct. The India-English sample exhibited higher correlations, 0.56 and 0.67 for the seven image form and total form, respectively. These are in the range of the US data from Study 1, and indicate adequate evidence for convergent validity. The difference between the two Indian samples indicates that the translations might be at fault for the low levels of validity exhibited in the India-Hindi version and better translations might improve the results.

- The third question asked "Are the images, with the addition of text, generalizable across cultures?" The answer is yes. There were seven items that were investigated across the two cultures. Three of the seven were flagged as exhibiting DIF, while four items were not flagged. These results are an indication that there are images, with text included that can be developed for use across cultures, although the process of selecting those items might be challenging. Hopefully the results of these studies will provide more information for those trying to build these types of assessments.

## Summary of Studies 1 and 2

This chapter presented an example of developing a subtest of an instrument designed to measure personality, and to determine whether or not it is possible to identify images that could be used in different cultural contexts. Two cultures that were very different were used in the example to show that it is possible to identify images that can be culturally neutral and would function similarly across cultural contexts. Using more of the strategies to handle potential biases identified in Chapter 3 would likely lead to even better results. Employing as many of these strategies as possible is advised. This example was intended to be illustrative of the process that could be implemented to create, evaluate, and validate such an assessment. The value of finding culturally neutral images is high; creating such assessments would save time for the respondents, and both time and money for test developers.

With respect to the results of Study 2, the value of including text or not is not clear. This preliminary study indicated that while there were some benefits in including text with the images, there might also be some challenges that arise when the text is included. The quality of the translation in this case may have led to reduced validity evidence, reduced reliability, and less clear factor

*Figure 10.*

Take Home Tips

- Constructing a visual assessment is an iterative process
- Use experts from all relevant cultures to select initial images
- Use more images that you need
- Use data to inform the quality of the selection
- Refine measure based on the data

structure. However, the advantage that it offered in the US sample in terms of increased validity evidence, increased reliability and increased clarity in the factor structure is an indication that it might be worth exploring this option more carefully in the context of cross-cultural assessment. It is essential that a good translation of that text be used, even if the translation task appears to be simple. A final reminder that the data presented here is for one aspect of personality, and would be used in a larger complete assessment of personality that included similar measures for the other personality dimensions.

## SUMMARY

Creating an image-based assessment that is culturally-neutral is difficult. The two studies presented in this chapter highlight the difficulties in selecting images that will be interpreted similarly across two very different cultures. Including text along with the images did help. Text was translated and included, and was also presented in English, since English is widely spoken, to determine the impact that translation might have on the results. The results using the English rather than the translated text suggests that adding in the translation component might create additional difficulties. Therefore, finding images that might work well without text might be a better approach to constructing the assessment. Ultimately, images were found that were generalizable across cultures, although numerous images were tested to find those that were appropriate. This process would likely be simplified if some of the strategies included in Chapter 3 were utilize to limit the bias in the assessment.

# REFERENCES

Allport, G. W., & Odbert, H. S. (1936). Trait-names: A psycho-lexical study. *Psychological Monographs*, *47*(211).

Benet-Martínez, V., & John, O. P. (1998). Los Cinco Grandes across cultures and ethnic groups: Multitrait method analyses of the Big Five in Spanish and English. *Journal of Personality and Social Psychology*, *75*(3), 729–750. doi:10.1037/0022-3514.75.3.729 PMID:9781409

Bieda, A., Hirschfeld, G., Schönfeld, P., Brailovskaia, J., Zhang, X. C., & Margraf, J. (2016). Universal happiness? Cross-cultural measurement invariance of scales assessing positive mental health. *Psychological Assessment*. doi:10.1037/pas0000353 PMID:27322203

Borgatta, E. F. (1964). The structure of personality characteristics. *Behavioral Science*, *12*(1), 8–17. doi:10.1002/bs.3830090103 PMID:14204891

Bresciani, S., & Eppler, M. J. (2010a, July). Choosing Knowledge Visualizations to Augment Cognition: The Manager's View. *IEEE Proceedings of the 14th International Conference Information Visualization*. London, UK: IEEE.

Bresciani, S., & Eppler, M. J. (2010b). Glocalizaing visual communication in organizations. In B. Bertagni, M. La Rosa, & F. Salvetti (Eds.), *Glocal working* (pp. 233–251). Milan: Franco Angeli.

Buhrmester, M., Kwang, T., & Gosling, S. D. (2011). Amazons Mechanical Turk: A new source of inexpensive, yet high-quality, data? *Perspectives on Psychological Science*, *6*, 3–5. doi:10.1177/1745691610393980 PMID:26162106

Byrne, B. M., & van de Vijver, F. R. (2010). Testing for Measurement and Structural Equivalence in Large-Scale Cross-Cultural Studies: Addressing the Issue of Nonequivalence. *International Journal of Testing*, *10*(2), 107–132. doi:10.1080/15305051003637306

Chamorro-Premuzic, T., & Ahmetoglu, G. (2013). *Personality 101*. Springer.

Costa, P. T. Jr, & McCrae, R. R. (1985). *The NEO Personality Inventory manual*. Odessa, FL: Psychological Assessment Resources.

Creed, P. A., Patton, W., & Watson, M. B. (2002). Cross-Cultural equivalence of the Career Decision-Making Self-Efficacy Scale-Short Form: An Australian and South African comparison. *Journal of Career Assessment*, *10*(3), 327–342. doi:10.1177/10672702010003004

Denissen, J. J. A., Geenen, R., van Aken, M. A. G., Gosling, S. D., & Potter, J. (2008). Development and validation of a Dutch translation of the Big Five Inventory (BFI). *Journal of Personality Assessment*, *90*(2), 152–157. doi:10.1080/00223890701845229 PMID:18444109

Digman, J. M., & Takemolo-Chock, N. K. (1981). Factors in the natural language of personality: Re-analysis. comparison. and interpretation of six major studies. *Multivariate Behavioral Research*, *6*(2), 149–170. doi:10.1207/s15327906mbr1602_2 PMID:26825420

Fiske, D. W. (1949). Consistency of the factorial structures of personality ratings from different sources. *Journal of Abnormal and Social Psychology*, *44*(3), 329–344. doi:10.1037/h0057198 PMID:18146776

Furukawa, T. A., Streiner, D. L., Azuma, H., Higuchi, T., Kamijima, K., Kanba, S., & Miura, S. et al. (2005). Cross-cultural equivalence in depression assessment: Japan-Europe-North American study. *Acta Psychiatrica Scandinavica*, *112*(4), 279–285. doi:10.1111/j.1600-0447.2005.00587.x PMID:16156835

Hochwalder, J. (2006). A psychometric assessment of a Swedish translation of Shafers personality scale. *Scandinavian Journal of Psychology*, *47*(6), 523–530. doi:10.1111/j.1467-9450.2006.00524.x PMID:17107501

Ipeirotis, P. G. (2010). Demographics of Mechanical Turk (Tech. Rep. No. CeDER-10-01). New York: New York University. Available http://hdl.handle.net/2451/29585

John, O. P. & Srivastava, S. (2008). The Big-Five Trait Taxonomy: History, Measurement, and Theoretical Perspectives. In L. Pervin & O.P. John (Eds.), *Handbook of personality: Theory and research* (2nd ed.). New York: Guilford.

Kankaraš, M., & Moors, G. (2014). Analysis of cross-cultural comparability of pisa 2009 scores. *Journal of Cross-Cultural Psychology*, *45*(3), 381–399. doi:10.1177/0022022113511297

Kim, S. H., Cohen, A. S., & Park, T. H. (1995). Detection of differential item functioning in multiple groups. *Journal of Educational Measurement, 32*(3), 261–276. doi:10.1111/j.1745-3984.1995.tb00466.x

Kulas, J. T., Thompson, R. C., & Anderson, M. G. (2011). California Psychological Inventory Dominance Scale measurement equivalence: General population Normative and Indian, U.K., and U.S. managerial samples. *Educational and Psychological Measurement, 71*(1), 245–257. doi:10.1177/0013164410391580

Leung, D. Y., Wong, E. M., Chan, S. S., & Lam, T. H. (2013). Psychometric properties of the Big Five Inventory in a Chinese sample of smokers receiving cessation treatment: A validation study. *Journal of Nursing Education and Practice, 3*(6). doi:10.5430/jnep.v3n6p1

Leung, D. Y. P., Wong, E. M. L., Chan, S. S. C., & Lam, T. H. (2012). Psychometric properties of the BigFive Inventory in a Chinese sample of smokers receiving cessation treatment: A validation study. *Jounral of Nursing Education and Practice, 3*(6), 1–10.

Liu, Y., Millsap, R. E., West, S. G., Tein, J., Tanaka, R., & Grimm, K. J. (2016). Testing measurement invariance in longitudinal data with ordered-categorical measures. *Psychological Methods.* doi:10.1037/met0000075 PMID:27213981

Luk, J. W., King, K. M., McCarty, C. A., Vander Stoep, A., & McCauley, E. (2016). Measurement invariance testing of a three-factor model of parental warmth, psychological control, and knowledge across European and Asian/Pacific Islander American youth. *Asian American Journal of Psychology, 7*(2), 97–107. doi:10.1037/aap0000040 PMID:27347358

Lynn, R., & Martin, T. (1995). National differences for thirty-seven nations in extraversion, neuroticism, psychoticism and economic, demographic and other correlates. *Personality and Individual Differences, 19*(3), 403–406. doi:10.1016/0191-8869(95)00054-A

Milfont, T. L., & Fischer, R. (2010). Testing measurement invariance across groups: Applications in cross-cultural research. *International Journal of Psychological Research, 3*(1), 111–121.

Mlacic, B., & Goldberg, L. R. (2007). An analysis of a cross-cultural personality inventory: The IPIP Big-Five Factor Measure in Croatia. *Journal of Personality Assessment*, *88*(2), 168–177. doi:10.1080/00223890701267993 PMID:17437382

Muck, P., Hell, B., & Gosling, S. D. (2007). Construct validation of a short five-factor model instrument-a self-peer study on the German adaptation of the ten-item personality inventory (TIPI-G). *European Journal of Psychological Assessment*, *23*(3), 166–175. doi:10.1027/1015-5759.23.3.166

Norman, W. T. (1963). Toward an adequate taxonomy of personality attributes: Replicated factor structure in peer nomination personality ratings. *Journal of Abnormal and Social Psychology*, *66*(6), 574–583. doi:10.1037/h0040291 PMID:13938947

Rammstedt, B., & John, O. P. (2007). Measuring personality in one minute orless: A 10-item short version of the Big Five Inventory in English and German. *Journal of Research in Personality*, *41*(1), 2003–2212. doi:10.1016/j.jrp.2006.02.001

Schmitt, D. P., Allik, J., McCrae, R. R., & Benet-Martínez, V. (2007). The geographic distribution of Big Five personality traits: Pattern and profiles of human self-description across 56 nations. *Journal of Cross-Cultural Psychology*, *38*(2), 173–212. doi:10.1177/0022022106297299

Suacier, G. (1994). Mini-markers: A brief version of Goldbergs unipolar Big-Five markers. *Journal of Personality Assessment*, *63*(3), 506–516. doi:10.1207/s15327752jpa6303_8 PMID:7844738

Thompson, E. R. (2008). Development and validation of an international English Big-Five mini markers. *Personality and Individual Differences*, *45*(6), 542–548. doi:10.1016/j.paid.2008.06.013

Traitify. (2016). *Personality assessments for every audience*. Retrieved from https://www.traitify.com/assessments/

Tupes, E. C., & Chrislal, R. E. (1961). *Recurrent personality factors based on trait ratings* (USAF ASD Tech. Rep. No. 61-97). L.ackland Air Force Base, TX: U.S. Air Force.

Ubbiali, A., Chiorri, C., Hampton, P., & Donati, D. (2013). Psychometric properties of the Italian adaptation of the Big Five Inventory (BFI). *Bollettino di Psicologia Applicata*, *266*, 37–46.

Visual DNA. (2016). *Using Visual Questionnaires to Measure Personality Traits*. Academic Press.

Wasti, S. A., Tan, H. H., Brower, H. H., & Önder, Ç. (2007). Cross-cultural measurement of supervisor trustworthiness: An assessment of measurement invariance across three cultures. *The Leadership Quarterly*, *18*(5), 477–489. doi:10.1016/j.leaqua.2007.07.004

Wasti, S. A., Tan, H. H., Brower, H. H., & Önder, Ç. (2007). Cross-cultural measurement of supervisor trustworthiness: An assessment of measurement invariance across three cultures. *The Leadership Quarterly*, *18*(5), 477–489. doi:10.1016/j.leaqua.2007.07.004

Weiss, T., & Berger, R. (2006). Reliability and validity of a Spanish version of the Posttraumatic Growth Inventory. *Research on Social Work Practice*, *16*(2), 191–199. doi:10.1177/1049731505281374

Whisman, M. A., & Judd, C. M. (2016). A cross-national analysis of measurement invariance of the Satisfaction With Life Scale. *Psychological Assessment*, *28*(2), 239–244. doi:10.1037/pas0000181 PMID:26168309

Woods, C. M. (2009). Evaluation of MIMIC-model methods for DIF testing with comparison to two-groups analysis. *Multivariate Behavioral Research*, *44*(1), 1–27. doi:10.1080/00273170802620121 PMID:26795105

Wu, W., Lu, Y., Tan, F., Yao, S., Steca, P., Abela, J. Z., & Hankin, B. L. (2012). Assessing measurement invariance of the Childrens Depression Inventory in Chinese and Italian primary school student samples. *Assessment*, *19*(4), 506–516. doi:10.1177/1073191111421286 PMID:21911438

Xu, F., Hilpert, P., Randall, A. K., Li, Q., & Bodenmann, G. (2016). Validation of the Dyadic Coping Inventory with Chinese couples: Factorial structure, measurement invariance, and construct validity. *Psychological Assessment*, *28*(8), e127–e140. doi:10.1037/pas0000329 PMID:27183045

Yildirim, H. H., & Berberoglu, G. (2009). Judgmental and statistical DIF analyses of the pisa-2003 mathematics literacy items. *International Journal of Testing*, *9*(2), 108–121. doi:10.1080/15305050902880736

Yuan, K., & Chan, W. (2016). Measurement Invariance via Multigroup SEM: Issues and Solutions With Chi-Square-Difference Tests. *Psychological Methods*, *21*(3), 405–426. doi:10.1037/met0000080 PMID:27266799

# Chapter 6
# Conclusions and Future Directions

## ABSTRACT

*Chapter 6 contains the lessons learned in the construction, development and evaluation of the visual assessment developed in Chapter 5, which were the application of the concepts presented in Chapters 1-4. Along with the conclusions of that research, ideas for future research to potentially enhance visual assessments are provided. The conclusion of the book details the promise and hope for visual assessments and the need for much more research in this area.*

## INTRODUCTION

When this project began, it was unknown how well images could generalize across cultures. Hand gestures and facial expressions mean different things in different countries. Colors mean different things in different cultures. Further, research even suggests that we notice different features in different images, and even see colors themselves differently. If this is true, how could it be possible to select images that would elicit the same type of responses across samples of people who live in different cultures? While only one type of personality measure has been examined, a very limited example, the results are promising. In Study 1, of the eight items chosen to represent this construct, five of them generalized across two cultures, and in Study 2, four

DOI: 10.4018/978-1-5225-2691-9.ch006

of the seven generalized across the two cultures. This result is promising, especially as the images chosen were chosen with an American audience in mind, and not thinking about how the appearance of the subjects in the pictures would be perceived in another country. The results of this very limited study are promising. Perhaps cultural differences aren't as impenetrable as we sometimes think, and it is possible to find images that people of very different cultures can see in the same way.

While the results of this investigation are quite promising, there is no doubt that it is preliminary. A measure has been constructed that focuses on one aspect of personality: extroversion. It would be foolhardy to generalize these results to any other type of visual assessment. Some constructs will be more difficult to represent pictorially, for example, and some of the images that seem appropriate might be harder to generalize across samples. It is impossible to know without conducting more research to determine how difficult the task will be.

In addition to representing a limited construct, only two cultures were considered in this example. While we did make an effort to choose cultures that might have differences, it is impossible to know if the same images would generalize to other cultures. It may be that the images that generalize across these two cultures are not the same images that would generalize across another two cultures. This is new territory, and more research is required to determine how universal images are across different cultures. There are cultures that are likely more similar than others; many European cultures probably share cultural norms that would make generalizability across those cultures easier, than say generalizing from European to Asian cultures. Determining equivalency across cultures will be an enormous task, however, the task will be relatively straightforward when compared to the task of translating text into multiple languages, still needing to take care of cultural aspects of the text.

This research has definitely just touched the tip of the iceberg in determining how generalizable visual assessments might be. This area of research is still in its infancy. Given the prevalence of these types of "quizzes" on social media, the power of images as compared to words, the ease of producing and administering visual assessments in a way that was just not possible until recently, we believe that these types of assessments will be very valuable and important in the future. As such, research in this area will be quite important as we continue to delve into the world of image-based assessments and their generalizability across cultures.

# FUTURE DIRECTIONS

As previously mentioned, we have yet to even scrape the tip of the iceberg with respect to the research on visual assessments, and there is still plenty of work to be done. Some thoughts on what might be next steps are discussed.

## Expert Judgment

One aspect of selecting images that would generalize across cultures that we were not able to explore here was the use of expert judgment. A lot of work could be saved if experts from the different cultures were able to react to the images for selection purposes. In this way, the expert judgment would decrease a step in the process of having to use empirical data to determine whether or not an image would be perceived in the same way in a different culture. It is not necessarily true that the experts would be 100% accurate in their judgments of course, as one or two people could not possibly represent the range of opinions of a particular culture; however, it would reduce the possible images to a smaller subset so that the data collection could be limited to images that are more likely to generalize across cultures.

In addition to help select the final images, the experts could also be used to provide insight into why they made the choices that the made. By gathering this type of information, images for future assessments could be selected keeping these guidelines in mind. For example, pointing the index finger at a person is not uncommon in the United States, but it is considered offensive in many cultures (Cotton, 2013). Knowing this, images with this gesture can be avoided not only in the assessment currently being constructed, for which the expert was hired, but also for all future assessments that might be constructed. That is to say, there is an opportunity to learn from one another about how different cultures experience the world. The greater the knowledge we gain, the easier it will be to create visual assessments that will be generalizable across cultures.

This approach was used in the development of the International English Mini Markers version of the Big Five Inventory. Adjectives that were identified as not generalizable across cultures could be replaced with adjectives that were clearer across the different cultures, enhancing the validity and the reliability of the resulting instrument. While quantitative data are often given great credence, it cannot answer the question of *why* the results were observed; we need humans to provide that piece of the picture. Therefore, both qualitative and quantitative data should be used to develop visual assessments to increase the likelihood that the images will generalize across the cultures of interest.

## Response Options

In the text-based version of the Big Five personality inventory, the response options are a range of answers: "Strongly Agree, Somewhat Agree, Neutral, Somewhat Disagree, Strongly Disagree." In contrast, with the visual assessment developed here, the response options were only "Like Me" or "Not Like Me" which forces respondents to choose one side of the continuum, unlike the 5 point response option, where degrees of how much the respondents agree with the statement are possible. This simplification to "Like Me" and "Not Like Me" might lead to several challenges. One challenge is just in the nature of the data that would result. With only two response options, the variability in the data is necessarily reduced. In the text-based instrument, each of the eight items has five response categories, so the total score range is 8-40. In contrast, for eight image-based items, with only two response categories, the possible score range is 8-16. This restricted range provides less opportunity for differentiating people along a continuum of extroversion, as compared to the larger scale of the text-based questions. Increasing the number of response options for the picture could rectify this situation. For example, options could be, "A Lot Like Me" "Somewhat Like Me" "Neutral" "Not Really Like Me" and "Not at All Like Me." The disadvantage to using five categories might be (1) there is more text to translate, and the language is a little more nuanced, creating more potential for miscommunication in the translated versions of the assessment, (2) the assessment takes longer, as the cognitive load and decision making activity of the respondent is higher, and (3) the instrument becomes a bit more cumbersome. A compromise might be to use 3 categories: "A Lot Like Me," "Somewhat Like Me," and "Not At All Like Me." Using more categories would increase the score range, and increase the potential for uncovering the variability in the respondents.

Using two response options of "Like Me" or "Not Like Me" also forces the respondents to choose one side of the continuum on which to place themselves. It is an all-or-nothing proposition. Most people are not completely introverts, or completely extroverts, but lie somewhere along the continuum. By using the two response options, in essence the continuum is reduced to the two ends. By restriction options for the respondents, it might be more difficult for the respondents to choose the option that is most like them. If this choice is made more difficult, then the resulting data is less likely to be reflective of the personality characteristics of the respondent. Adding additional response options might provide the opportunity for the respondents to feel more comfortable about placing themselves along the continuum, and the responses might be more consistent with the personality trait that is being measured.

## Using Images and Text

Like in Study 2, the option of adding text to the images should be explored further, given the positive results in the US sample. While our goal was initially to keep the instrument as text-free as possible, and use only images, there might be an advantage to combining text and images. One company, Traitify (Reviewed in Chapter 2), does create visual assessments, although each image also includes some text. For example, an image might include text like "Energized By Others" along with the image of a group of people celebrating together (Traitify, 2016). The text provides a context by which the respondent should interpret the image. Therefore, there is less risk of the respondent interpreting the text in a way that was not intended. For example, instead of thinking about "Energized by Others" the respondent might think the image is about "Enjoys Parties." A person might be energized by others, but does not enjoy parties. Therefore, the way that the image is interpreted will have an impact on the choice of "Like Me" or "Not Like Me."

We initially made the choice to not include text on the images very deliberately so as to minimize the need for translation/literacy, and rely only on what the image elicits in the respondent. This choice most likely led to responses that are based on interpretations of the images that were not intended. For example, as mentioned in Chapter 4, when choosing pictures representing extroversion, several images had sports imagery to depict motion and excitement. However, the analysis of the responses clearly revealed that there was something affecting responses that was not related to extroversion. It is likely that those pictures were being interpreted as "athletic" or "enjoys sports" or "active." By not including text with the image, more care has to be taken about contexts other than the intended contexts that might confuse the measurement of the construct of interest. From a practical perspective, it likely means trying out more images to find the correct set of images to use. However, the caution of the impact of a potentially poor translation was also illustrated in Study 2. Therefore, the benefits and trade-offs of using such an approach should be investigated further, as it is not clear what is the best approach.

Other ways of using text should also be explored. In BuzzFeed quizzes, the questions are traditional multiple-choice questions with text-based stems and answers. However, images are provided for each. As an example a question might be "How do you like your eggs?" This is accompanied by the image of a breakfast table. The response options are, as expected, "over easy," "scrambled," "poached," "over-hard," "sunny side up," and "I don't like eggs." For each of these options there is an image of the type of egg. While this might not be a purely image-based assessment, using the images in conjunction with the words can have many advantages. The processing of the two types of information is different, and some might process some types information better than other types of information; by including both, you are including both types of people. More importantly, perhaps, when it comes to cross-cultural assessments, if the text is translated poorly, then the images help the respondent understand what the text might mean. The images might help with the interpretation of the text, and the text might help with the interpretation of the images. This strategy might offer some exciting advantages.

## Types of Images

In the studies presented here, the images were all photos chosen from available royalty-free websites (e.g. Shutterstock.com). While this option is the most convenient and cost-effective, it does entail some limitations, as compared to other options that offer more flexibility. These options include creating your own images; the images created by yourself could be photos, drawings, or computer-generated images. When creating images purposefully the use in the assessment, the image can be created to include only what is wanted, and nothing more. When using premade images, whether photos or other images, the image may include extraneous background, or might not be composed ideally for the message that is being conveyed. This lack of flexibility in using existing items can make it more challenging to have culturally neutral images. The features of images that are culturally influenced can't be manipulated when choosing from pre-existing images. For example, color has specific cultural meanings. If the image is found, rather than created, then there is no ability to control the colors in the image. Similarly for the context of a photo: when the photo exists, any background context might change the interpretation of the photo in different cultures; if the photo is created for the purposes of the assessment, much greater control can be exercised over the features that are influenced by culture.

Another option for images is whether photographs are used, or non-photographic images, which might include drawings or computer-generated images. When using symbols, it is natural that the visual image is not a photograph, but is either a drawing or a computer-generated image. Drawings (either by hand, or computer) and photos each have their advantages as well as their limitations. Photos provide a realistic image, and as noted in Qi (2013), factual information was more easily communicated through imagery than symbolic information. While the purpose of the photo might not be to convey factual information, using a photo might have some advantage because it is realistic, and the experience portrayed in the image might be less ambiguous across cultures. The challenges that arise with photos is that they might be harder to control and manipulate than drawings. Suppose the goal was to produce images in several different colors, to determine the impact of color on the interpretation of the image. It might be easier to do this with drawings than with photos. Creating drawings of people that are culturally neutral might be easier since line drawings of people might evoke less cultural interpretation. Skin tone, hair and eye color, and shapes of features, can be more abstract and ambiguous in a drawing as opposed to a photo, where real people have a particular skin tone, hair or eye color that cannot be denied. The only way to manipulate this feature in photos is to have people of different skin tones, hair and eye color, which might be difficult to obtain.

While the idea of constructing items made of images might seem relatively straightforward, there are many issues that need to be considered, including those included here. Because there is limited research regarding how these different choices are perceived across cultures, there is little guidance available in how to make these choices, and future research can explore these ideas.

## Number of Images

In the studies presented here only one image was presented and the respondent reacted to that image. While offering explanatory text might help to direct the focus of the respondent to what the image is trying to convey, in so doing, text is added to the assessment. Since one of the features of visual assessments is the lack of a need to translate text, adding text is a potential drawback, even if the text is simple. Another option is to provide more than one image, and have the respondent choose which is more like him/her. For example, when measuring extraversion, two images could be presented: a person with a group of people having fun, and a person doing the same activity, but alone. The respondent could then choose which image they identify with more. In providing the two contrasting images, it might make it clearer what the person should be focusing on in the image. This idea could be expanded to include more than two images as well, since it may not be a binary trait. Some might enjoy small groups of people, but not large groups, and prefer the small group to being alone. These three scenarios could be presented as a set, with the respondent choosing the image that is most "like" them. In a sense, this is extending the idea of a multiple point scale, where the scale is in the images themselves, instead of in the response to a single image. This approach of presenting multiple images is the approach used in many of the online, non-scientifically designed quizzes that are ubiquitous on the Internet.

In the context of a personality assessment, and many other assessments, the idea of using multiple images could simplify the assessment. For the full Big Five Inventory, a large number of images could be presented to the respondent and he/she could choose all of the images that are "like me." There is no reason to provide a prompt for each image, since the current set up is to indicate "like me" (Zickuhr &Rainie, 2014) or "not like me" for each image. It would be more efficient to provide a set of images and give one direction of choosing all images that are "like me" As each image does not require a response. Additionally, in this design, there is also no "not like me" option, keeping all responses in the positive, which may offer some advantages.

## Images as Answer Options

Visual assessments could include text-based questions, and image-based responses. This approach is used in the Visual DNA versions of the image-based personality measures. A prompt like "How would you most like to spend your day?" is followed by a series of images, and the respondent chooses the image that represents what they would like most to do. It would be interesting to see how these types of visual assessments compare to other types of visual assessments such as those presented here.

## Adaptive Assessments

All of the innovation proposed is in changing from text to image; however, the basic form of the assessment has not been changed. The quizzes online, and the assessments that have been made by Traitify, or VisualDNA, or the ones proposed here, all utilize a traditional multiple-choice type format, presented in a static delivery mode. However, the most modern text-based assessments being produced utilize adaptive technology. By including some kind of adaptivity, the power of the visual assessment could be even greater. As noted in the top 10 Internet quizzes, the more personalized the quiz, the more popular (Haynam, 2014). Adaptivity could result in more personalized assessments, and hence more engaging and powerful assessments. This adaptivity could take many forms, and could help address some of the issues associated with features that do not generalize across cultures, such as context, symbol, or color. Some of the options are provided here.

## Context

Adaptive testing with text usually means that the items are individually chosen to be presented to the person taking the assessment. That is, not all people experience the same questions on the test, but the items are tailored to the ability of the person. This idea could be extended to visual assessments as well. Sticking with the example of a personality assessment, and specifically, measuring extraversion, images could be presented based on the images that the person selects as "like them." If the person is choosing mostly images that indicate extraversion, more images geared toward extraversion could be presented to be sure that it is what they are identifying with. These additional items might present different contexts, to be sure that the person is not merely responding too much to the context of the picture, but with the trait being measured. If the respondent chooses "like me" for many images depicting extraversion in multiple situations, that is additional evidence regarding the level of extraversion the person exhibits. Further, the person might have extraverted tendencies in some contexts but not others, so if the person does not identify with the extraverted image in a context, the introverted option in the same context could be provided, if it is available. For example, if a person is generally choosing images displaying extraversion, and then an image is displayed of many people playing a sport together, perhaps running together in a large group, and the person does not identify with that particular image, it may be that the person does not enjoy running, or the person prefers to run solo. This can be teased apart, if desired, but then showing an image of a person running alone. IF the person identifies with that image, it could be that the person enjoys sports alone, while generally prefers to be with others. This is one simple example of how the adaptive selection of images might work.

## Symbol

It is clear that there is symbolic language that varies across culture. Consider the symbol for peace. A common symbol in Western cultures appears as shown in Figure 1.

While it may seem universal, in Indian cultures, a symbol of peace looks like that images presented in Figure 2.

If an image of peace would be desirable to use in the visual assessment, there is not likely a universal symbol for peace. However, the choice of symbols could be made depending upon who is responding to the assessment. By providing some simple demographic information at the start of the assessment, choices of which symbol should be used in the image could be made, and adapted to the culture of the respondent. While this strategy is not resulting in a universal design for a visual assessment that can be used across cultures, it could harness technology to address the difficulties of finding truly culturally neutral images, and allow for different versions of the test to exist, just as a translation would. Alternately, it would not be necessary to choose only one image for peace to be demonstrated. Imagine a person identifying as Indian in the initial questions; the second peace symbol would be chosen for that person. However, suppose that person has been living in Europe most of their

*Figure 1.*

*Figure 2.*

life, and would be more familiar with the peace figure shown in Figure 1. It could be possible for the respondent to click, "show different image" and have the alternate image shown. In this way, each person could be exposed to the different possible scenarios, where appropriate, to provide the best information possible to assess him or her.

## Color

Similar to symbols, images featuring different color options could be available, and depending on the person taking the assessment, the image chosen could fit the culture most appropriately. So, if a person is identifying as Chinese, the "Eastern Color Images" could be presented. Conversely, if the person identifies as English, the "Western Color Images" could be chosen. In this way, the power of color can be harnessed to evoke emotion, which would likely enhance the power of the image in assessment. This may provide a better alternative to using colors that are more culturally neutral, where the power of color is essentially eliminated from the image. The risk of trying to be culturally neutral is that all of the power of imagery that is inherent to cultures is lost. It is important to be culturally neutral if the same images are presented across cultures. However, given the power of technology to make changes at the individual level, there may be a way to have an assessment that is valid across cultures and still retains the power of the cultural images, symbols and colors. Images are largely powerful because of the symbolic nature of many aspects of culture, so to be able to retain the ability to invoke cultural symbolism, while being appropriate across cultures might be a better solution.

## Personal Characteristics

Because people identify more with images that look like themselves, images that include people could also be customized to the culture. That is, if the respondent is Asian, Asian people could appear in the images, and if the person is Indian, Indian people could appear in the images. This could be customized at any level that the designer chooses, with culture, gender, hair and eye color. The finer the customization, the more versions of the images that would have to exist in the image bank, so the limitations are largely practical, not technical.

## Interactive

While adaptivity does provide a more flexible platform for administering the assessments, and could make them more powerful, the assessments would still largely look like traditional multiple-choice questions. There is nothing wrong with multiple-choice questions, and they are certainly efficient and effective tools for measuring many traits. However, the key to these newer innovative assessments is to be more engaging, and perhaps through that engagement, better measurement is gained. One possible alternative is to make the assessments more interactive and less passive. Many approaches could be taken to increase interactivity and engagement. Provided here are some potential options.

## Video

Images are still, and hence more passive. Adding video clips might be even more exciting, and might help to provide more information in a quick way. The videos could include sound, but might not. It would be wise to minimize conversation or words spoken in the videos, as the point is to minimize text for translation, and spoken word would also need to be translated. However, scenarios can be illustrated in video without sound. For example, for measuring extraversion, two video clips might be used: in the first, a person could be home and get a phone call; he/she listens and smiles and leaves the house and meets up with friends at a café. In the second video, the person is home, gets a phone call, shakes his/her head, and leaves the house to go the movies alone; he/she gets popcorn, sits down and smiles as the movie starts. In the first video, clearly the person is choosing to be with a group of people while the second is choosing to be alone; in addition, in both cases the person is leaving the house to go do something, and what varies is what the person chooses to do. These scenarios might be more informative than just a still of a picture of someone out with friends, or a still of a picture of someone at the movies, as the action of choosing is included.

It was noted before that movement and activity and action were more associated with extraversion as opposed to introversion. This would be much easier to convey through video, where movement is possible than through still images. Fast-paced, fast-moving, scenarios could be presented, and slow, serene scenarios could be presented easily through video.

If audio is used, one indicator of extraversion/introversion could be the level of noise that is involved in the situation. Extraverts might be more comfortable in loud places where there are people, while introverts prefer quiet. This could be more easily communicated with video where the sound is a variable that can be manipulated. The main point is that visual does not need to mean static images, although that is the status today. Visual is visual. It could be static; it could be video. Using the best medium to convey what it needed should be chosen, and any visual medium is likely to lead to higher engagement.

## Interactive Items

Multiple-choice type items are not very interactive. The respondent simple chooses the response, or responses, that are the correct answer. This is not the only type of item that could be used in an assessment, and in particular, in a visual assessment. There are examples of assessments that people have to construct images, including the House-Tree-Person (HTP) projective personality assessment (Buck & Warren, 1992) that has been used to assess potential personality disorders. In the HTP Assessment, the person is required to draw a picture of each object (house, tree, person) and then they are asked questions about their drawings. This type of assessment is much more interactive, but also much more time-intensive. With the use of computers, and graphic tools and pre-made images, however, this could be streamlined in a non-projective test. Consider the short prompt: Create your perfect day. This simple text would need to be translated, of course. Then the person is provided a large set of images that they could choose as elements of a perfect day. Each element could be tagged as indicating an "extraverted image" or an "introverted image" so that the final complete image could be easily scored. While there is much more that would need to be done to validate this type of assessment, since it is very novel, it might provide far more information than traditional selected response items through the engagement and purposeful action of the respondent. While images could be selected at random, it is less likely that a chaotic image be constructed than it is for a person to randomly answer multiple-choice questions. Elements of the image could include different sized groups of people that could be chosen, different activities, etc.

The assessment could take the form of a video game, like SIMCITY, or such types of games. In these games, the respondent goes through their day and different scenarios arise, and the respondent would have to react to the situation. For example, to continue the introvert/extravert example, the person could be at home, and they build the home how they would like it. Then perhaps people move in with them, and does the respondent choose to build more walls or rooms, or live more communally. Are the living quarters made more separate or is there shared space. Once they leave the house, they walk down the street, and encounter friends. Do they choose to go alone with the friends, or do they choose to continue on their own? A simulated day could be made to see how the person reacts to constructed events that would be aimed at differentiating introverts and extraverts. The respondent would likely be very engaged in this activity, and would not even feel as if they are taking an assessment. Given the high engagement factor, and the potential for variations, the simulation could be replicated across multiple occasions to measure the trait on different days, or at different times.

## Avatar

This final type of interactivity could be combined with some of the other features given above, either in the customization in the adaptivity section, or with the interactive item types. People could choose an avatar of themselves that is used in the images. They could also choose avatars of friends. Many apps and video games take advantage of using avatars to represent the person playing the game. This could be included in the assessment design to help with the customization of the assessment, but also the personalization of the assessment, which could lead to greater interest and engagement. By blurring the lines between games and assessments, our greatest gains can be made in engagement and perhaps lead to more authentic assessment.

## Assessing the Equivalence Across Cultures

In addition to work on the creation and use of visual assessment in cross-cultural contexts, research related to how to evaluate the equivalence of the assessments across cultures is also necessary. In any analysis that in investigating the differential functioning of items across groups, one of the biggest challenges is finding a criterion on which to match the two groups. Since the analysis requires that the groups be matched on the construct of interest, the most typical situation is to use the total score on the instrument that is being evaluated. In many situations, this is not very problematic, since there is likely to be very few items identified as potentially showing some differential performance across the groups. There are situations where it is trickier. One of the most notable examples is when language is a problem. For an instrument that is not designed to measure literacy, the impact of literacy on the resulting score is likely to be large if there is any text to be read to respond to the instrument. Using the instrument to match the two groups being compared will be problematic because if one group has lower literacy (e.g. non-native speakers), the scores on the test will not be truly representative of the trait of interest, and will be contaminated by the literacy effect. That situation is similar to this situation, even though we have eliminated the dependence on literacy. Since there is very little known about the functioning of the items in different cultures, it is difficult to know if the matching of the groups using the responses to images is an appropriate indicator of the trait being measured. One option is to use a matching variable that is external to the instrument being studied. Since the goal of this project is to adapt an existing text-based assessment into a visual assessment, it would be possible to use scores on the text-based assessment, which has been validated in several cultures (McCrae, 2002), as the matching variable. Using such an approach might provide better insight into the equivalence of the images across the different cultures.

## SUMMARY

The field of image-based assessment is in its infancy. Even more so the aspect of creating such assessments that can be used globally. With the world shrinking with the use of technology, it is essential that efforts be made to investigate methods to create these types of assessments that can be used across cultures. Multiple suggestions for future development of image-based assessments, either for one or more cultures, were provided and include utilizing technology to make the assessments adaptable. By adapting the assessment to the user, features of images, such as those discussed in Chapter 2, could be selected for the appropriate culture of the person, making the assessments more accessible to people of different cultures. There is much work left to do to understand how these assessments work and how to adapt them sufficiently to be culturally neutral.

There is great promise in the use of visual assessments across cultures. The advantages of such assessments are clear, and the appeal of such assessments is likely to exceed that of traditional text-based assessments. While there is much work to be done to understand the development of such assessments, and the limitations of the generalizability across different populations and subgroups, the results of this preliminary investigation shows great hope that there is enough commonality among people of different cultures to be able to find images that transcend culture. The greater difficulty might not be in the cross-cultural equivalence, but in the development of the assessments themselves. With the ubiquity of social media, cultures are linked in ways that

*Figure 3.*

*Figure 4.*

> **Take Home Tips**
>
> - Visual assessments hold promise for cross-cultural assessment
> - There is a lot that remains to figure out
> - Computer adaptation offers promise
> - These are the wave of the future for assessments

they have not been before, breaking down barriers between cultures. These types of assessments are likely to be part of a next generation of assessments, targeting a generation that is more technologically oriented, with more visual experience. We cannot wait to see what the future holds.

# REFERENCES

Buck, J. N., & Warren, W. L. (1992). The House-Tree-Person projective drawing technique: Manual and interpretive guide. Los Angeles, CA: Western Psychological Services.

Cotton, G. (2013, August 13). *Gestures to avoid in cross-cultural business: In other words, 'Keep your fingers to yourself!'*. Retrieved from http://www. huffingtonpost.com/gayle-cotton/cross-cultural-gestures_b_3437653.html

Haynam, J. (2014, November 4). *What the top 100 most viewed interact quizzes all have in common* [Interact Blog]. Retrieved from https://www. tryinteract.com/blog/what-the-top-100-most-viewed-interact-quizzes-all-have-in-common/

McCrae, R. R. (2002). Cross-Cultural Research on the Five-Factor Model of Personality. *Online Readings in Psychology and Culture*, 4(4). doi:10.9707/2307-0919.1038

Traitify. (2016). *Personality assessments for every audience*. Retrieved from https://www.traitify.com/assessments/

Zickuhr, K., & Rainie, L. (2014, September 10). *Younger Americans and Public Libraries*. Retrieved from http://www.pewinternet.org/2014/09/10/younger-americans-and-public-libraries/

# Appendix

## ITEMS IN BIG FIVE INVENTORY

I see myself as someone who

…is talkative
…tends to find fault with others
…does a thorough job
…is depressed
…is original, comes up with new ideas
…is reserved
…is helpful and unselfish with others
…can be somewhat careless
…is relaxed, handles stress well
…is curious about many things
…is full of energy
…starts quarrels with others
…is a reliable worker
…can be tense
…is ingenious, a deep thinker
…generates lots of enthusiasm
…has a forgiving nature
…tends to be disorganized
…worries a lot
…has an active imagination
…tends to be quiet
…is generally trusting
…tends to be lazy
…is emotionally stable, not easily upset
…is inventive

...has an assertive personality

...can be cold and aloof

...perseveres until the task is finished

...can be moody

...values artistic, aesthetic experiences

...is sometimes shy, inhibited

...is considerate and kind to almost everyone

...does things efficiently

...remains calm in tense situations

...prefers work that is routine

...is outgoing, sociable

...is sometimes rude to others

...makes plans and follows through with them

...gets nervous easily

...likes to reflect, play with ideas

...has few artistic interests

...likes to cooperate with others

...is easily distracted

...is sophisticated in art, music, or literature

...is politically liberal

...has high self esteem

# Related Readings

To continue IGI Global's long-standing tradition of advancing innovation through emerging research, please find below a compiled list of recommended IGI Global book chapters and journal articles in the areas of assessment development, visual literacy, and visual media. These related readings will provide additional information and guidance to further enrich your knowledge and assist you with your own research.

Adera, B. (2017). Supporting Language and Literacy Development for English Language Learners. In J. Keengwe (Ed.), *Handbook of Research on Promoting Cross-Cultural Competence and Social Justice in Teacher Education* (pp. 339–354). Hershey, PA: IGI Global. doi:10.4018/978-1-5225-0897-7.ch018

Alexander, A., & Schlemmer, R. H. (2017). The Convergence of Critical Pedagogy with Arts-Based Service-Learning. In R. Shin (Ed.), *Convergence of Contemporary Art, Visual Culture, and Global Civic Engagement* (pp. 1–23). Hershey, PA: IGI Global. doi:10.4018/978-1-5225-1665-1.ch001

Alisat, L., & Clarke, V. B. (2017). An Integral Analysis of Labeling, Inclusion, and the Impact of the K-12 School Experience on Gifted Boys. In J. Keengwe (Ed.), *Handbook of Research on Promoting Cross-Cultural Competence and Social Justice in Teacher Education* (pp. 355–381). Hershey, PA: IGI Global. doi:10.4018/978-1-5225-0897-7.ch019

Baughan, P. (2017). Demonstrating Positive, Learner-Centred Assessment Practice in Professional Development Programmes. In E. Cano & G. Ion (Eds.), *Innovative Practices for Higher Education Assessment and Measurement* (pp. 333–347). Hershey, PA: IGI Global. doi:10.4018/978-1-5225-0531-0.ch017

Bazler, J. A. (2017). Tower Design as a STEAM Project. In J. Bazler & M. Van Sickle (Eds.), *Cases on STEAM Education in Practice* (pp. 206–219). Hershey, PA: IGI Global. doi:10.4018/978-1-5225-2334-5.ch010

Berner, A. (2015). AiryLight: Ambient Environmental Data. In A. Ursyn (Ed.), *Handbook of Research on Maximizing Cognitive Learning through Knowledge Visualization* (pp. 487–492). Hershey, PA: IGI Global. doi:10.4018/978-1-4666-8142-2.ch017

Bright, A., & Gambrell, J. (2017). Calling In, Not Calling Out: A Critical Race Framework for Nurturing Cross-Cultural Alliances in Teacher Candidates. In J. Keengwe (Ed.), *Handbook of Research on Promoting Cross-Cultural Competence and Social Justice in Teacher Education* (pp. 217–235). Hershey, PA: IGI Global. doi:10.4018/978-1-5225-0897-7.ch011

Brown, V. (2016). Creating Global Classrooms Using Universal Design for Learning. In M. Yildiz & J. Keengwe (Eds.), *Handbook of Research on Media Literacy in the Digital Age* (pp. 186–207). Hershey, PA: IGI Global. doi:10.4018/978-1-4666-9667-9.ch009

Brzezicki, M. (2015). Simultaneous Perception of Parallel Streams of Visual Data. In A. Ursyn (Ed.), *Handbook of Research on Maximizing Cognitive Learning through Knowledge Visualization* (pp. 84–101). Hershey, PA: IGI Global. doi:10.4018/978-1-4666-8142-2.ch003

Burbach, J. H., Martin, S. B., Arnold-Fowlkes, J., Sakaith, J., Julius, C., & Hibbs, A. (2017). This Is How I Learn: Co-Creating Space for Students' Voices. In J. Keengwe (Ed.), *Handbook of Research on Promoting Cross-Cultural Competence and Social Justice in Teacher Education* (pp. 178–192). Hershey, PA: IGI Global. doi:10.4018/978-1-5225-0897-7.ch009

Burgess, C. M., & Evans, J. R. (2017). Culturally Responsive Relationships Focused Pedagogies: The Key to Quality Teaching and Creating Quality Learning Environments. In J. Keengwe (Ed.), *Handbook of Research on Promoting Cross-Cultural Competence and Social Justice in Teacher Education* (pp. 1–31). Hershey, PA: IGI Global. doi:10.4018/978-1-5225-0897-7.ch001

Burtin, A. S., Hampton-Garland, P., & Mizelle-Johnson, N. (2017). "I Don't See Color, I Grade on Content": An Approach to Addressing Embodied Microaggressive Behaviors in Preservice Teacher Programs. In J. Keengwe (Ed.), *Handbook of Research on Promoting Cross-Cultural Competence and Social Justice in Teacher Education* (pp. 236–252). Hershey, PA: IGI Global. doi:10.4018/978-1-5225-0897-7.ch012

Byker, E. J. (2016). Assessing Experience: Performance-Based Assessment of Experiential Learning Activities. In D. Polly (Ed.), *Evaluating Teacher Education Programs through Performance-Based Assessments* (pp. 261–280). Hershey, PA: IGI Global. doi:10.4018/978-1-4666-9929-8.ch016

Cardoso, E. O., Bricaire, J. M., Hurtado, F. B., & Mendoza, J. G. (2016). Evaluation Results of Initial Training Teachers Programs in Mexico Based on the Performance of Their Students. In D. Polly (Ed.), *Evaluating Teacher Education Programs through Performance-Based Assessments* (pp. 311–327). Hershey, PA: IGI Global. doi:10.4018/978-1-4666-9929-8.ch019

Carver, M. (2017). Feedback, Feedforward, or Dialogue?: Defining a Model for Self-Regulated Learning. In E. Cano & G. Ion (Eds.), *Innovative Practices for Higher Education Assessment and Measurement* (pp. 1–18). Hershey, PA: IGI Global. doi:10.4018/978-1-5225-0531-0.ch001

Catelli, L. A., Carlino, J., Petraglia, G., Godek, P., & Jackson, V. (2016). Collaborative Video-Based Action Research Studies to Assess Classroom Teaching Performances and Improve Educator Programs: A Model Research Approach. In D. Polly (Ed.), *Evaluating Teacher Education Programs through Performance-Based Assessments* (pp. 295–310). Hershey, PA: IGI Global. doi:10.4018/978-1-4666-9929-8.ch018

Chen, A. Y. (2017). Demographic Imperativeness: Critical Issues in Preparing Minority Teacher Candidates in Teacher Education. In J. Keengwe (Ed.), *Handbook of Research on Promoting Cross-Cultural Competence and Social Justice in Teacher Education* (pp. 101–119). Hershey, PA: IGI Global. doi:10.4018/978-1-5225-0897-7.ch005

Chen, J. J. (2016). Educating English Language Learners for Success in the 21st Century: Facilitating Their Acquisition of Multiliteracies. In M. Yildiz & J. Keengwe (Eds.), *Handbook of Research on Media Literacy in the Digital Age* (pp. 75–90). Hershey, PA: IGI Global. doi:10.4018/978-1-4666-9667-9.ch004

Chen, M., & Su, F. (2017). Global Civic Engagement as an Empowering Device for Cross-Ethnic and Cross-Cultural Understanding in Taiwan. In R. Shin (Ed.), *Convergence of Contemporary Art, Visual Culture, and Global Civic Engagement* (pp. 24–45). Hershey, PA: IGI Global. doi:10.4018/978-1-5225-1665-1.ch002

Cintrón, R., & McLean, M. (2017). Purposeful Course Scheduling: Increasing Enrollment and Promoting Academic Progression. In R. Cintron, J. Samuel, & J. Hinson (Eds.), *Accelerated Opportunity Education Models and Practices* (pp. 100–121). Hershey, PA: IGI Global. doi:10.4018/978-1-5225-0528-0.ch005

Clausen, C. K. (2017). Exploring Technology Through Issues of Social Justice. In J. Keengwe (Ed.), *Handbook of Research on Promoting Cross-Cultural Competence and Social Justice in Teacher Education* (pp. 137–158). Hershey, PA: IGI Global. doi:10.4018/978-1-5225-0897-7.ch007

Cline, B. J. (2016). Media Ecology and the 21st Century Classroom. In M. Yildiz & J. Keengwe (Eds.), *Handbook of Research on Media Literacy in the Digital Age* (pp. 275–290). Hershey, PA: IGI Global. doi:10.4018/978-1-4666-9667-9.ch013

Coats, C. (2017). The Collective Aestheticization of Farming as Participatory Civic Engagement. In R. Shin (Ed.), *Convergence of Contemporary Art, Visual Culture, and Global Civic Engagement* (pp. 185–209). Hershey, PA: IGI Global. doi:10.4018/978-1-5225-1665-1.ch011

Constant, J. (2015). Random Processes and Visual Perception: Stochastic Art. In A. Ursyn (Ed.), *Handbook of Research on Maximizing Cognitive Learning through Knowledge Visualization* (pp. 200–212). Hershey, PA: IGI Global. doi:10.4018/978-1-4666-8142-2.ch006

Coupet, S. Q., & Nicolas, G. (2017). We Drank the Cola in Collaboration: Voices of Haitian Teachers in Haiti. In J. Keengwe (Ed.), *Handbook of Research on Promoting Cross-Cultural Competence and Social Justice in Teacher Education* (pp. 159–177). Hershey, PA: IGI Global. doi:10.4018/978-1-5225-0897-7.ch008

Crossley, J. G. (2017). Assessing the Non-Cognitive Domains: Measuring What Matters Well. In E. Cano & G. Ion (Eds.), *Innovative Practices for Higher Education Assessment and Measurement* (pp. 348–372). Hershey, PA: IGI Global. doi:10.4018/978-1-5225-0531-0.ch018

Cuthrell, K. C., Lys, D. B., Fogarty, E. A., & Dobson, E. E. (2016). Using edTPA Data to Improve Programs. In D. Polly (Ed.), *Evaluating Teacher Education Programs through Performance-Based Assessments* (pp. 67–79). Hershey, PA: IGI Global. doi:10.4018/978-1-4666-9929-8.ch005

de Burgh-Woodman, H. (2017). Student Perceptions of Value and the Impact on Curriculum Design: A Case Study. In R. Cintron, J. Samuel, & J. Hinson (Eds.), *Accelerated Opportunity Education Models and Practices* (pp. 1–33). Hershey, PA: IGI Global. doi:10.4018/978-1-5225-0528-0.ch001

DeMink-Carthew, J., Hyler, M. E., & Valli, L. (2016). Redesigning Teacher Education in the Context of Multiple Reform Initiatives. In D. Polly (Ed.), *Evaluating Teacher Education Programs through Performance-Based Assessments* (pp. 1–17). Hershey, PA: IGI Global. doi:10.4018/978-1-4666-9929-8.ch001

Di Blas, N. (2016). 21st Century Skills and Digital Storytelling in the Classroom. In M. Yildiz & J. Keengwe (Eds.), *Handbook of Research on Media Literacy in the Digital Age* (pp. 306–330). Hershey, PA: IGI Global. doi:10.4018/978-1-4666-9667-9.ch015

DiBiase, W. J., McDonald, J. R., & Strong, K. (2017). Constructing a Marshmallow Catapult. In J. Bazler & M. Van Sickle (Eds.), *Cases on STEAM Education in Practice* (pp. 260–276). Hershey, PA: IGI Global. doi:10.4018/978-1-5225-2334-5.ch013

Djoub, Z. (2017). Assessment for Learning: Feeding Back and Feeding Forward. In E. Cano & G. Ion (Eds.), *Innovative Practices for Higher Education Assessment and Measurement* (pp. 19–35). Hershey, PA: IGI Global. doi:10.4018/978-1-5225-0531-0.ch002

Dollahon, C. V. (2017). Using STEAM in Marine Science: Incorporating Graphic Design Into an Existing STEM Lesson. In J. Bazler & M. Van Sickle (Eds.), *Cases on STEAM Education in Practice* (pp. 292–317). Hershey, PA: IGI Global. doi:10.4018/978-1-5225-2334-5.ch015

Donohue, P. J., & Kelly, K. (2016). Transforming Digital Literacy with Culturally Diverse, Personalized Learning. In M. Yildiz & J. Keengwe (Eds.), *Handbook of Research on Media Literacy in the Digital Age* (pp. 161–185). Hershey, PA: IGI Global. doi:10.4018/978-1-4666-9667-9.ch008

Ebrahimi, A. (2015). Visual Plan Construct Language (VPCL): Visual System and Method for Teaching and Learning Programming and Problem Solving through Knowledge Visualization. In A. Ursyn (Ed.), *Handbook of Research on Maximizing Cognitive Learning through Knowledge Visualization* (pp. 326–343). Hershey, PA: IGI Global. doi:10.4018/978-1-4666-8142-2.ch010

Eca, T. T., Saldanha, A., & Franco, A. M. (2017). "Insurgence": Activism in Art Education Research and Praxis. In R. Shin (Ed.), *Convergence of Contemporary Art, Visual Culture, and Global Civic Engagement* (pp. 210–223). Hershey, PA: IGI Global. doi:10.4018/978-1-5225-1665-1.ch012

Eisenberg, M., & Eisenberg, A. (2015). Sensory Extension as a Tool for Cognitive Learning. In A. Ursyn (Ed.), *Handbook of Research on Maximizing Cognitive Learning through Knowledge Visualization* (pp. 72–83). Hershey, PA: IGI Global. doi:10.4018/978-1-4666-8142-2.ch002

El-Henawy, W. M. (2017). Assessment Techniques in EFL Brain-Compatible Classroom. In E. Cano & G. Ion (Eds.), *Innovative Practices for Higher Education Assessment and Measurement* (pp. 79–100). Hershey, PA: IGI Global. doi:10.4018/978-1-5225-0531-0.ch005

Estes, J. S. (2017). Preparing Teacher Candidates for Diverse Classrooms: The Role of Teacher Preparation Programs. In J. Keengwe (Ed.), *Handbook of Research on Promoting Cross-Cultural Competence and Social Justice in Teacher Education* (pp. 52–75). Hershey, PA: IGI Global. doi:10.4018/978-1-5225-0897-7.ch003

Fattal, L. R. (2017). Catastrophe: An Uncanny Catalyst for Creativity. In R. Shin (Ed.), *Convergence of Contemporary Art, Visual Culture, and Global Civic Engagement* (pp. 244–262). Hershey, PA: IGI Global. doi:10.4018/978-1-5225-1665-1.ch014

Fernández-Ferrer, M., & Pons-Seguí, L. (2017). Feedforward. The Key to Improve Learning in Higher Education. In E. Cano & G. Ion (Eds.), *Innovative Practices for Higher Education Assessment and Measurement* (pp. 188–206). Hershey, PA: IGI Global. doi:10.4018/978-1-5225-0531-0.ch010

Finson, K. D. (2017). Finding and Using the ART in Science Lessons. In J. Bazler & M. Van Sickle (Eds.), *Cases on STEAM Education in Practice* (pp. 183–205). Hershey, PA: IGI Global. doi:10.4018/978-1-5225-2334-5.ch009

Flannery, M. C. (2015). Science of the Archives: Visual Learning about Plants. In A. Ursyn (Ed.), *Handbook of Research on Maximizing Cognitive Learning through Knowledge Visualization* (pp. 213–241). Hershey, PA: IGI Global. doi:10.4018/978-1-4666-8142-2.ch007

Fleming, J., & Kajimoto, M. (2016). The Freedom of Critical Thinking: Examining Efforts to Teach American News Literacy Principles in Hong Kong, Vietnam, and Malaysia. In M. Yildiz & J. Keengwe (Eds.), *Handbook of Research on Media Literacy in the Digital Age* (pp. 208–235). Hershey, PA: IGI Global. doi:10.4018/978-1-4666-9667-9.ch010

Fondrie, S., Penick-Parks, M., & Delano-Oriaran, O. (2017). Developing Equity Literacy through Diverse Literature for Children and Young Adults. In J. Keengwe (Ed.), *Handbook of Research on Promoting Cross-Cultural Competence and Social Justice in Teacher Education* (pp. 193–216). Hershey, PA: IGI Global. doi:10.4018/978-1-5225-0897-7.ch010

Friesem, Y. (2016). Developing Digital Empathy: A Holistic Approach to Media Literacy Research Methods. In M. Yildiz & J. Keengwe (Eds.), *Handbook of Research on Media Literacy in the Digital Age* (pp. 145–160). Hershey, PA: IGI Global. doi:10.4018/978-1-4666-9667-9.ch007

Funk, S., Kellner, D., & Share, J. (2016). Critical Media Literacy as Transformative Pedagogy. In M. Yildiz & J. Keengwe (Eds.), *Handbook of Research on Media Literacy in the Digital Age* (pp. 1–30). Hershey, PA: IGI Global. doi:10.4018/978-1-4666-9667-9.ch001

Gallo, P., & Coelho, M. D. (2016). Pedagogical Guidelines to Introduce Transmedia Learning into the Classroom: The Brazilian Context. In M. Yildiz & J. Keengwe (Eds.), *Handbook of Research on Media Literacy in the Digital Age* (pp. 331–350). Hershey, PA: IGI Global. doi:10.4018/978-1-4666-9667-9.ch016

Graybill, L. (2017). Using Air to Move Paper Airplanes and Balloon Rockets: The Great Race. In J. Bazler & M. Van Sickle (Eds.), *Cases on STEAM Education in Practice* (pp. 220–246). Hershey, PA: IGI Global. doi:10.4018/978-1-5225-2334-5.ch011

Greenblatt, D. (2016). Supporting Teacher Candidates Completing the edTPA. In D. Polly (Ed.), *Evaluating Teacher Education Programs through Performance-Based Assessments* (pp. 184–200). Hershey, PA: IGI Global. doi:10.4018/978-1-4666-9929-8.ch012

Groff, C. A. (2017). High-Quality Trade Books and Content Areas: Planning Accordingly for Rich Instruction. In J. Bazler & M. Van Sickle (Eds.), *Cases on STEAM Education in Practice* (pp. 38–52). Hershey, PA: IGI Global. doi:10.4018/978-1-5225-2334-5.ch003

Guàrdia, L., Crisp, G., & Alsina, I. (2017). Trends and Challenges of E-Assessment to Enhance Student Learning in Higher Education. In E. Cano & G. Ion (Eds.), *Innovative Practices for Higher Education Assessment and Measurement* (pp. 36–56). Hershey, PA: IGI Global. doi:10.4018/978-1-5225-0531-0.ch003

Hamer, R., & Jan van Rossum, E. (2017). Students' Conceptions of Understanding and Its Assessment. In E. Cano & G. Ion (Eds.), *Innovative Practices for Higher Education Assessment and Measurement* (pp. 140–161). Hershey, PA: IGI Global. doi:10.4018/978-1-5225-0531-0.ch008

Han, H. S. (2017). The Third Culture: The Transforming (Visual) Culture in Globalized Virtual Worlds. In R. Shin (Ed.), *Convergence of Contemporary Art, Visual Culture, and Global Civic Engagement* (pp. 318–330). Hershey, PA: IGI Global. doi:10.4018/978-1-5225-1665-1.ch018

Hart, L. C., & Wakeman, S. (2016). Creating Faculty Buy-In for edTPA and Other Performance-Based Assessments. In D. Polly (Ed.), *Evaluating Teacher Education Programs through Performance-Based Assessments* (pp. 80–92). Hershey, PA: IGI Global. doi:10.4018/978-1-4666-9929-8.ch006

Hartman, J. D. (2017). Glocalism: Situating Global Civic Engagement in the Local Community. In R. Shin (Ed.), *Convergence of Contemporary Art, Visual Culture, and Global Civic Engagement* (pp. 151–169). Hershey, PA: IGI Global. doi:10.4018/978-1-5225-1665-1.ch009

Heafner, T. L. (2016). Teacher Effect Model for Impacting Student Achievement. In D. Polly (Ed.), *Evaluating Teacher Education Programs through Performance-Based Assessments* (pp. 376–392). Hershey, PA: IGI Global. doi:10.4018/978-1-4666-9929-8.ch022

Henderson, L. K. (2017). Meltdown at Fukushima: Global Catastrophic Events, Visual Literacy, and Art Education. In R. Shin (Ed.), *Convergence of Contemporary Art, Visual Culture, and Global Civic Engagement* (pp. 80–99). Hershey, PA: IGI Global. doi:10.4018/978-1-5225-1665-1.ch005

Hsieh, K. (2017). Authentic Art and Cultural Learning Overseas: Developing Students' Global and Intercultural Competencies through a Study Abroad Program in China. In R. Shin (Ed.), *Convergence of Contemporary Art, Visual Culture, and Global Civic Engagement* (pp. 138–149). Hershey, PA: IGI Global. doi:10.4018/978-1-5225-1665-1.ch008

Hunzicker, J. L., Arquette, C. M., Olson, P., & Atkins, D. (2016). Using a Literacy-Based Classroom Partnership to Prepare Teacher Candidates for the edTPA. In D. Polly (Ed.), *Evaluating Teacher Education Programs through Performance-Based Assessments* (pp. 237–259). Hershey, PA: IGI Global. doi:10.4018/978-1-4666-9929-8.ch015

Ibarra-Sáiz, M. S., & Rodriguez-Gomez, G. (2017). Serious Games for Students' E-Assessment Literacy in Higher Education. In E. Cano & G. Ion (Eds.), *Innovative Practices for Higher Education Assessment and Measurement* (pp. 271–294). Hershey, PA: IGI Global. doi:10.4018/978-1-5225-0531-0.ch014

Idrissi, M. K., Hnida, M., & Bennani, S. (2017). Competency-Based Assessment: From Conceptual Model to Operational Tool. In E. Cano & G. Ion (Eds.), *Innovative Practices for Higher Education Assessment and Measurement* (pp. 57–78). Hershey, PA: IGI Global. doi:10.4018/978-1-5225-0531-0.ch004

Iftimescu, S., Iucu, R., Marin, E., & Stîngu, M. M. (2017). Authentic Assessment: An Inquiry into the Assessment Process at Master's Degree Level. In E. Cano & G. Ion (Eds.), *Innovative Practices for Higher Education Assessment and Measurement* (pp. 373–391). Hershey, PA: IGI Global. doi:10.4018/978-1-5225-0531-0.ch019

Jablon, P. C. (2017). Theater as the STEAM Engine for Engaging Those Previously Disengaged. In J. Bazler & M. Van Sickle (Eds.), *Cases on STEAM Education in Practice* (pp. 118–153). Hershey, PA: IGI Global. doi:10.4018/978-1-5225-2334-5.ch006

Jamieson, H. V. (2017). We have a Situation!: Cyberformance and Civic Engagement in Post-Democracy. In R. Shin (Ed.), *Convergence of Contemporary Art, Visual Culture, and Global Civic Engagement* (pp. 297–317). Hershey, PA: IGI Global. doi:10.4018/978-1-5225-1665-1.ch017

Karadag, Z., & Devecioglu-Kaymakci, Y. (2016). Cognitive Approach to Improve Media Literacy: Mind Puzzles. In M. Yildiz & J. Keengwe (Eds.), *Handbook of Research on Media Literacy in the Digital Age* (pp. 351–373). Hershey, PA: IGI Global. doi:10.4018/978-1-4666-9667-9.ch017

Kasemsap, K. (2017). Encouraging Continuing Professional Development and Teacher Professional Development in Global Education. In R. Cintron, J. Samuel, & J. Hinson (Eds.), *Accelerated Opportunity Education Models and Practices* (pp. 168–202). Hershey, PA: IGI Global. doi:10.4018/978-1-5225-0528-0.ch008

Kato, Y., & Kato, S. (2016). Mobile Phone Use during Class at a Japanese Women's College. In M. Yildiz & J. Keengwe (Eds.), *Handbook of Research on Media Literacy in the Digital Age* (pp. 436–455). Hershey, PA: IGI Global. doi:10.4018/978-1-4666-9667-9.ch021

Keifer-Boyd, K. T. (2017). FemTechNet Distributed Open Collaborative Course: Performing Difference, Exquisite Engendering, and Feminist Mapping. In R. Shin (Ed.), *Convergence of Contemporary Art, Visual Culture, and Global Civic Engagement* (pp. 278–296). Hershey, PA: IGI Global. doi:10.4018/978-1-5225-1665-1.ch016

Kim, J. H. (2016). Pedagogical Approaches to Media Literacy Education in the United States. In M. Yildiz & J. Keengwe (Eds.), *Handbook of Research on Media Literacy in the Digital Age* (pp. 53–74). Hershey, PA: IGI Global. doi:10.4018/978-1-4666-9667-9.ch003

Knochel, A. D. (2017). Ground Control to Major Tom: Satellite Seeing, GPS Drawing, and (Outer)Space. In R. Shin (Ed.), *Convergence of Contemporary Art, Visual Culture, and Global Civic Engagement* (pp. 264–277). Hershey, PA: IGI Global. doi:10.4018/978-1-5225-1665-1.ch015

Koester, M. (2017). Getting to "Know" STEAM. In J. Bazler & M. Van Sickle (Eds.), *Cases on STEAM Education in Practice* (pp. 53–85). Hershey, PA: IGI Global. doi:10.4018/978-1-5225-2334-5.ch004

Labadie, J. A. (2015). Digitally Mediated Art Inspired by Scientific Research: A Personal Journey. In A. Ursyn (Ed.), *Handbook of Research on Maximizing Cognitive Learning through Knowledge Visualization* (pp. 436–471). Hershey, PA: IGI Global. doi:10.4018/978-1-4666-8142-2.ch015

Lachance, J. (2016). Portfolios: TESL Candidates' Transformed Understandings of Portfolio Assessments with English Learners through Performance-Based Assessment. In D. Polly (Ed.), *Evaluating Teacher Education Programs through Performance-Based Assessments* (pp. 166–183). Hershey, PA: IGI Global. doi:10.4018/978-1-4666-9929-8.ch011

LaRocca, C. K. (2017). Academic Advising and Student Persistence: Understanding the Role of Academic Advising and Connection to Student Persistence. In R. Cintron, J. Samuel, & J. Hinson (Eds.), *Accelerated Opportunity Education Models and Practices* (pp. 51–73). Hershey, PA: IGI Global. doi:10.4018/978-1-5225-0528-0.ch003

Lee, T., & Lim, D. H. (2017). International Faculty Development in U.S. Higher Education. In J. Keengwe (Ed.), *Handbook of Research on Promoting Cross-Cultural Competence and Social Justice in Teacher Education* (pp. 304–319). Hershey, PA: IGI Global. doi:10.4018/978-1-5225-0897-7.ch016

Lehning, H. (2015). Visualization and Mathematical Thinking. In A. Ursyn (Ed.), *Handbook of Research on Maximizing Cognitive Learning through Knowledge Visualization* (pp. 103–112). Hershey, PA: IGI Global. doi:10.4018/978-1-4666-8142-2.ch004

Lesterhuis, M., Verhavert, S., Coertjens, L., Donche, V., & De Maeyer, S. (2017). Comparative Judgement as a Promising Alternative to Score Competences. In E. Cano & G. Ion (Eds.), *Innovative Practices for Higher Education Assessment and Measurement* (pp. 119–138). Hershey, PA: IGI Global. doi:10.4018/978-1-5225-0531-0.ch007

Liccardo, A., & Grimes, C. (2015). Building a Computer. In A. Ursyn (Ed.), *Handbook of Research on Maximizing Cognitive Learning through Knowledge Visualization* (pp. 312–325). Hershey, PA: IGI Global. doi:10.4018/978-1-4666-8142-2.ch009

Lillie, J., & Jones-Lillie, M. (2015). Analyzing Disney's Early Exhibits as Installation Art Work. In A. Ursyn (Ed.), *Handbook of Research on Maximizing Cognitive Learning through Knowledge Visualization* (pp. 415–434). Hershey, PA: IGI Global. doi:10.4018/978-1-4666-8142-2.ch014

Lim, W., & Lischka, A. E. (2016). Examination of Content Validity for edTPA: Academic Language and Representation. In D. Polly (Ed.), *Evaluating Teacher Education Programs through Performance-Based Assessments* (pp. 109–124). Hershey, PA: IGI Global. doi:10.4018/978-1-4666-9929-8.ch008

Lindquist, W. P., James-Hassan, M., & Lindquist, N. C. (2017). Exploring Simple Machines With Creative Movement. In J. Bazler & M. Van Sickle (Eds.), *Cases on STEAM Education in Practice* (pp. 86–117). Hershey, PA: IGI Global. doi:10.4018/978-1-5225-2334-5.ch005

Lopez, A. E., & Olan, E. L. (2017). Critical Practices for Teaching and Learning in Global Contexts: Building Bridges for Action. In R. Shin (Ed.), *Convergence of Contemporary Art, Visual Culture, and Global Civic Engagement* (pp. 46–62). Hershey, PA: IGI Global. doi:10.4018/978-1-5225-1665-1.ch003

Lys, D. B., L'Esperance, M., Bullock, A., Dobson, E., Patriarca, L. A., & Maynard, E. E. (2016). Data and Dialogue: Cultivating Transformative Change in Teacher Preparation Programs. In D. Polly (Ed.), *Evaluating Teacher Education Programs through Performance-Based Assessments* (pp. 34–51). Hershey, PA: IGI Global. doi:10.4018/978-1-4666-9929-8.ch003

Mahajan, I. M., Rather, M., Shafiq, H., & Qadri, U. (2016). Media Literacy Organizations. In M. Yildiz & J. Keengwe (Eds.), *Handbook of Research on Media Literacy in the Digital Age* (pp. 236–248). Hershey, PA: IGI Global. doi:10.4018/978-1-4666-9667-9.ch011

Manzoor, A. (2016). Media Literacy in the Digital Age: Literacy Projects and Organizations. In M. Yildiz & J. Keengwe (Eds.), *Handbook of Research on Media Literacy in the Digital Age* (pp. 249–274). Hershey, PA: IGI Global. doi:10.4018/978-1-4666-9667-9.ch012

Mariano, G., Hammonds, F., Chambers, S., & Spear, G. (2017). Formative Evaluations of Teaching: Involving Students in the Assessment Process. In E. Cano & G. Ion (Eds.), *Innovative Practices for Higher Education Assessment and Measurement* (pp. 101–118). Hershey, PA: IGI Global. doi:10.4018/978-1-5225-0531-0.ch006

Martínez-Cerdá, J., Torrent-Sellens, J., & Caprino, M. P. (2016). Media Literacy, Co-Innovation, and Productivity: Examples from European Countries. In M. Yildiz & J. Keengwe (Eds.), *Handbook of Research on Media Literacy in the Digital Age* (pp. 374–404). Hershey, PA: IGI Global. doi:10.4018/978-1-4666-9667-9.ch018

Martono, F., & Salam, U. (2017). Students Learning in Asynchronous Discussion Forums: A Meta-Analysis. *International Journal of Information and Communication Technology Education*, *13*(1), 48–60. doi:10.4018/IJICTE.2017010105

McIntyre, C. J., Cartwright, A., & Miller, S. C. (2016). Process vs. Product: What Are Preservice Teachers Learning from ISL Projects? In D. Polly (Ed.), *Evaluating Teacher Education Programs through Performance-Based Assessments* (pp. 328–336). Hershey, PA: IGI Global. doi:10.4018/978-1-4666-9929-8.ch020

McNeal, K. (2016). Using Media Literacy to Teach and Learn the English Language Arts/Literacy: Common Core State Standards. In M. Yildiz & J. Keengwe (Eds.), *Handbook of Research on Media Literacy in the Digital Age* (pp. 291–305). Hershey, PA: IGI Global. doi:10.4018/978-1-4666-9667-9. ch014

Mejías, E., & Monereo, C. (2017). As Life Itself: Authentic Teaching and Evaluation of Professional Consulting Competencies in a Psychology Course. In E. Cano & G. Ion (Eds.), *Innovative Practices for Higher Education Assessment and Measurement* (pp. 311–332). Hershey, PA: IGI Global. doi:10.4018/978-1-5225-0531-0.ch016

Miraglia, K. M. (2017). Learning in Situ: Situated Cognition and Culture Learning in a Study Abroad Program. In R. Shin (Ed.), *Convergence of Contemporary Art, Visual Culture, and Global Civic Engagement* (pp. 118–137). Hershey, PA: IGI Global. doi:10.4018/978-1-5225-1665-1.ch007

Moran, R., Keith, K., & Hong, H. (2016). One University's Pathway to a Change in Practice. In D. Polly (Ed.), *Evaluating Teacher Education Programs through Performance-Based Assessments* (pp. 52–66). Hershey, PA: IGI Global. doi:10.4018/978-1-4666-9929-8.ch004

Moreira dos Anjos-Santos, L., El Kadri, M. S., Gamero, R., & Gimenez, T. (2016). Developing English Language Teachers' Professional Capacities through Digital and Media Literacies: A Brazilian Perspective. In M. Yildiz & J. Keengwe (Eds.), *Handbook of Research on Media Literacy in the Digital Age* (pp. 91–114). Hershey, PA: IGI Global. doi:10.4018/978-1-4666-9667-9.ch005

Morgan, B. M. (2017). Bridging the L1-L2 Divide: Learner-Centered Instruction in the Heritage/L2 Spanish Classroom. In J. Keengwe (Ed.), *Handbook of Research on Promoting Cross-Cultural Competence and Social Justice in Teacher Education* (pp. 270–286). Hershey, PA: IGI Global. doi:10.4018/978-1-5225-0897-7.ch014

Mysore, A. R. (2017). Teacher Education and Digital Equity: Research in the Millennium. In J. Keengwe (Ed.), *Handbook of Research on Promoting Cross-Cultural Competence and Social Justice in Teacher Education* (pp. 120–136). Hershey, PA: IGI Global. doi:10.4018/978-1-5225-0897-7.ch006

Nkabinde, Z. P. (2017). Multiculturalism in Special Education: Perspectives of Minority Children in Urban Schools. In J. Keengwe (Ed.), *Handbook of Research on Promoting Cross-Cultural Competence and Social Justice in Teacher Education* (pp. 382–397). Hershey, PA: IGI Global. doi:10.4018/978-1-5225-0897-7.ch020

Nogueiras, G., Herrero, D., & Iborra, A. (2017). Teaching for Epistemological Change: Self-Direction through Self-Assessment. In E. Cano & G. Ion (Eds.), *Innovative Practices for Higher Education Assessment and Measurement* (pp. 207–225). Hershey, PA: IGI Global. doi:10.4018/978-1-5225-0531-0.ch011

Osinska, V., Osinski, G., & Kwiatkowska, A. B. (2015). Visualization in Learning: Perception, Aesthetics, and Pragmatism. In A. Ursyn (Ed.), *Handbook of Research on Maximizing Cognitive Learning through Knowledge Visualization* (pp. 381–414). Hershey, PA: IGI Global. doi:10.4018/978-1-4666-8142-2.ch013

Paitz, K., Briggs, J., Lomasney, K., & Schneider, A. (2017). Juan Angel Chávez's Winded Rainbow: A Vehicle for Global Discussion and Local Action. In R. Shin (Ed.), *Convergence of Contemporary Art, Visual Culture, and Global Civic Engagement* (pp. 224–243). Hershey, PA: IGI Global. doi:10.4018/978-1-5225-1665-1.ch013

Panke, S. (2017). Designing Assessment, Assessing Instructional Design: From Pedagogical Concepts to Practical Applications. In E. Cano & G. Ion (Eds.), *Innovative Practices for Higher Education Assessment and Measurement* (pp. 296–310). Hershey, PA: IGI Global. doi:10.4018/978-1-5225-0531-0.ch015

Pedings-Behling, K. E. (2017). A Mathematical Approach to Designing Insulators. In J. Bazler & M. Van Sickle (Eds.), *Cases on STEAM Education in Practice* (pp. 247–259). Hershey, PA: IGI Global. doi:10.4018/978-1-5225-2334-5.ch012

Penland, J. L. (2017). Developing Resilience through Experiences: El Camino Al Exito. In J. Keengwe (Ed.), *Handbook of Research on Promoting Cross-Cultural Competence and Social Justice in Teacher Education* (pp. 287–303). Hershey, PA: IGI Global. doi:10.4018/978-1-5225-0897-7.ch015

*Related Readings*

Pereira, A., Tinoca, L., & Oliveira, I. (2017). Peer assessment in an Online Context: What Do Students Say? In E. Cano & G. Ion (Eds.), *Innovative Practices for Higher Education Assessment and Measurement* (pp. 248–270). Hershey, PA: IGI Global. doi:10.4018/978-1-5225-0531-0.ch013

Pereira, L. (2016). How to Use Parody and Humour to Teach Digital Literacy. In M. Yildiz & J. Keengwe (Eds.), *Handbook of Research on Media Literacy in the Digital Age* (pp. 423–435). Hershey, PA: IGI Global. doi:10.4018/978-1-4666-9667-9.ch020

Petty, T., Heafner, T. L., Lachance, J., & Polly, D. (2016). Supporting Teacher Education Candidates through the edTPA Process. In D. Polly (Ed.), *Evaluating Teacher Education Programs through Performance-Based Assessments* (pp. 201–216). Hershey, PA: IGI Global. doi:10.4018/978-1-4666-9929-8.ch013

Pinter, H. H., Winter, K. K., & Watson, M. K. (2016). How to Thrive in the Changing Landscape of Teacher Education: Planning for Implementation of Performance-Based Assessments. In D. Polly (Ed.), *Evaluating Teacher Education Programs through Performance-Based Assessments* (pp. 18–33). Hershey, PA: IGI Global. doi:10.4018/978-1-4666-9929-8.ch002

Pitre, N. J., & Clarke, V. B. (2017). Cultural Self-Study as a Tool for Critical Reflection and Learning: Integral Analysis and Implications for Pre-Service Teacher Education Programs. In J. Keengwe (Ed.), *Handbook of Research on Promoting Cross-Cultural Competence and Social Justice in Teacher Education* (pp. 76–100). Hershey, PA: IGI Global. doi:10.4018/978-1-5225-0897-7.ch004

Polly, D. (2016). Preparing Elementary Education Teacher Candidates to Design Learning Segments: The Case of edTPA Task One. In D. Polly (Ed.), *Evaluating Teacher Education Programs through Performance-Based Assessments* (pp. 126–137). Hershey, PA: IGI Global. doi:10.4018/978-1-4666-9929-8.ch009

Pyune, J. (2015). On Creativity of Asian and American Asian Students. In A. Ursyn (Ed.), *Handbook of Research on Maximizing Cognitive Learning through Knowledge Visualization* (pp. 472–486). Hershey, PA: IGI Global. doi:10.4018/978-1-4666-8142-2.ch016

Quesada, V., Garcia-Jimenez, E., & Gomez-Ruiz, M. A. (2017). Student Participation in Assessment Processes: A Way Forward. In E. Cano & G. Ion (Eds.), *Innovative Practices for Higher Education Assessment and Measurement* (pp. 226–247). Hershey, PA: IGI Global. doi:10.4018/978-1-5225-0531-0.ch012

Rademaker, S. M. (2016). Early and Often Creating and Implementing Performance-Based Field Instruments: For Students in Early Field Experiences. In D. Polly (Ed.), *Evaluating Teacher Education Programs through Performance-Based Assessments* (pp. 217–236). Hershey, PA: IGI Global. doi:10.4018/978-1-4666-9929-8.ch014

Ralston, N. C., & Hoffshire, M. (2017). An Individualized Approach to Student Transition: Developing a Success Coaching Model. In R. Cintron, J. Samuel, & J. Hinson (Eds.), *Accelerated Opportunity Education Models and Practices* (pp. 34–50). Hershey, PA: IGI Global. doi:10.4018/978-1-5225-0528-0.ch002

Redmond, T. A. (2016). Learning to Teach the Media: Pre-Service Teachers Articulate the Value of Media Literacy Education. In M. Yildiz & J. Keengwe (Eds.), *Handbook of Research on Media Literacy in the Digital Age* (pp. 31–52). Hershey, PA: IGI Global. doi:10.4018/978-1-4666-9667-9.ch002

Reis, Z. A. (2016). Bring the Media Literacy of Turkish Pre-Service Teachers to the Table. In M. Yildiz & J. Keengwe (Eds.), *Handbook of Research on Media Literacy in the Digital Age* (pp. 405–422). Hershey, PA: IGI Global. doi:10.4018/978-1-4666-9667-9.ch019

Rizzuto, K. C., Henning, J., & Duckett, C. (2017). Bee Pollination. In J. Bazler & M. Van Sickle (Eds.), *Cases on STEAM Education in Practice* (pp. 164–182). Hershey, PA: IGI Global. doi:10.4018/978-1-5225-2334-5.ch008

Rodríguez-de-Dios, I., & Igartua, J. (2016). Skills of Digital Literacy to Address the Risks of Interactive Communication. *Journal of Information Technology Research*, *9*(1), 54–64. doi:10.4018/JITR.2016010104

Romagnoli, A. (2017). Graphic Novels and STEAM: Strategies and Texts for Utilization in STEAM Education. In J. Bazler & M. Van Sickle (Eds.), *Cases on STEAM Education in Practice* (pp. 22–37). Hershey, PA: IGI Global. doi:10.4018/978-1-5225-2334-5.ch002

Rosenfeld, K. N. (2016). Terms of the Digital Age: Realities and Cultural Paradigms. In M. Yildiz & J. Keengwe (Eds.), *Handbook of Research on Media Literacy in the Digital Age* (pp. 115–144). Hershey, PA: IGI Global. doi:10.4018/978-1-4666-9667-9.ch006

Ryan, M. P. (2016). Lesson Study as an Effective Performance-Based Measure of Teacher Effectiveness. In D. Polly (Ed.), *Evaluating Teacher Education Programs through Performance-Based Assessments* (pp. 281–294). Hershey, PA: IGI Global. doi:10.4018/978-1-4666-9929-8.ch017

Seelke, J. L., & Mills, K. (2016). edTPA Local Evaluation: Engaging Our Partners, Improving Our Practice. In D. Polly (Ed.), Evaluating Teacher Education Programs through Performance-Based Assessments (pp. 93-108). Hershey, PA: IGI Global. doi:10.4018/978-1-4666-9929-8.ch007

Seiverd, K. (2017). "Imagioneering" a New Mission Space. In J. Bazler & M. Van Sickle (Eds.), *Cases on STEAM Education in Practice* (pp. 155–163). Hershey, PA: IGI Global. doi:10.4018/978-1-5225-2334-5.ch007

Semingson, P., & Amaro-Jiménez, C. (2017). Using Multimodal Literacies to Support Language Development for English Language Learners. In J. Keengwe (Ed.), *Handbook of Research on Promoting Cross-Cultural Competence and Social Justice in Teacher Education* (pp. 320–338). Hershey, PA: IGI Global. doi:10.4018/978-1-5225-0897-7.ch017

Servilio, K. L. (2017). Cases on STEAM Education in Practice: Differentiated Instruction. In J. Bazler & M. Van Sickle (Eds.), *Cases on STEAM Education in Practice* (pp. 319–334). Hershey, PA: IGI Global. doi:10.4018/978-1-5225-2334-5.ch016

Sharma, M. (2017). Activating Art Education Learning by Mapping Community Cultures. In R. Shin (Ed.), *Convergence of Contemporary Art, Visual Culture, and Global Civic Engagement* (pp. 170–184). Hershey, PA: IGI Global. doi:10.4018/978-1-5225-1665-1.ch010

Shipe, R. L. (2017). Productive Ambiguity: Promoting Cross-Cultural Understanding through Art. In R. Shin (Ed.), *Convergence of Contemporary Art, Visual Culture, and Global Civic Engagement* (pp. 63–79). Hershey, PA: IGI Global. doi:10.4018/978-1-5225-1665-1.ch004

Simmons, J. C. (2017). The Role of Social Media in the Globalized World of Education. In R. Cintron, J. Samuel, & J. Hinson (Eds.), *Accelerated Opportunity Education Models and Practices* (pp. 203–225). Hershey, PA: IGI Global. doi:10.4018/978-1-5225-0528-0.ch009

Smilan, C. (2017). The Art of Climate Change: Art Education for Global Citizenry. In R. Shin (Ed.), *Convergence of Contemporary Art, Visual Culture, and Global Civic Engagement* (pp. 100–117). Hershey, PA: IGI Global. doi:10.4018/978-1-5225-1665-1.ch006

Smith, S. B. (2017). Engineering and Art: Putting the EA in STEAM. In J. Bazler & M. Van Sickle (Eds.), *Cases on STEAM Education in Practice* (pp. 277–291). Hershey, PA: IGI Global. doi:10.4018/978-1-5225-2334-5.ch014

Starr-Glass, D. (2017). Prior Learning Assessment: Accelerating or Augmenting the College Degree? In R. Cintron, J. Samuel, & J. Hinson (Eds.), *Accelerated Opportunity Education Models and Practices* (pp. 226–258). Hershey, PA: IGI Global. doi:10.4018/978-1-5225-0528-0.ch010

Suleiman, R., & Byrd, C. (2016). edTPA Preparation: Building Support Structures for Teacher Candidates. In D. Polly (Ed.), Evaluating Teacher Education Programs through Performance-Based Assessments (pp. 138-165). Hershey, PA: IGI Global. doi:10.4018/978-1-4666-9929-8.ch010

Sweeny, R. W. (2017). The Politics of Video Games in STEM Education. In R. Shin (Ed.), *Convergence of Contemporary Art, Visual Culture, and Global Civic Engagement* (pp. 331–341). Hershey, PA: IGI Global. doi:10.4018/978-1-5225-1665-1.ch019

Taylor, P. G. (2015). What Does Learning Look Like?: Data Visualization of Art Teaching and Learning. In A. Ursyn (Ed.), *Handbook of Research on Maximizing Cognitive Learning through Knowledge Visualization* (pp. 494–514). Hershey, PA: IGI Global. doi:10.4018/978-1-4666-8142-2.ch018

Thomas, U. (2017). Disposition and Early Childhood Education Preservice Teachers: A Social Justice Stance. In J. Keengwe (Ed.), *Handbook of Research on Promoting Cross-Cultural Competence and Social Justice in Teacher Education* (pp. 253–269). Hershey, PA: IGI Global. doi:10.4018/978-1-5225-0897-7.ch013

Ulrich, C., & Ciolan, L. (2017). Beyond the Walls: Project-Based Learning and Assessment in Higher Education. In E. Cano & G. Ion (Eds.), *Innovative Practices for Higher Education Assessment and Measurement* (pp. 392–414). Hershey, PA: IGI Global. doi:10.4018/978-1-5225-0531-0.ch020

Ursyn, A. (2015). Cognitive Learning with Electronic Media and Social Networking. In A. Ursyn (Ed.), *Handbook of Research on Maximizing Cognitive Learning through Knowledge Visualization* (pp. 1–71). Hershey, PA: IGI Global. doi:10.4018/978-1-4666-8142-2.ch001

Ursyn, A. (2015). Duality of Natural and Technological Explanations. In A. Ursyn (Ed.), *Handbook of Research on Maximizing Cognitive Learning through Knowledge Visualization* (pp. 113–199). Hershey, PA: IGI Global. doi:10.4018/978-1-4666-8142-2.ch005

Ursyn, A., & Mostowfi, M. (2015). Visualization by Coding: Drawing Simple Shapes and Forms in Various Programming Languages. In A. Ursyn (Ed.), *Handbook of Research on Maximizing Cognitive Learning through Knowledge Visualization* (pp. 243–311). Hershey, PA: IGI Global. doi:10.4018/978-1-4666-8142-2.ch008

Van Sickle, M., & Koester, M. (2017). Musing on Unanswered Questions. In J. Bazler & M. Van Sickle (Eds.), *Cases on STEAM Education in Practice* (pp. 1–20). Hershey, PA: IGI Global. doi:10.4018/978-1-5225-2334-5.ch001

Velliaris, D. M., & Pierce, J. M. (2017). Personal and Professional Perceptions: Pre-University Pathway Programs, Pedagogy, and Praxis. In R. Cintron, J. Samuel, & J. Hinson (Eds.), *Accelerated Opportunity Education Models and Practices* (pp. 74–99). Hershey, PA: IGI Global. doi:10.4018/978-1-5225-0528-0.ch004

Viswanathan, R. (2017). Language Skills Training through Mobile Apps: Opportunities and Challenges. In R. Cintron, J. Samuel, & J. Hinson (Eds.), *Accelerated Opportunity Education Models and Practices* (pp. 142–167). Hershey, PA: IGI Global. doi:10.4018/978-1-5225-0528-0.ch007

Vorkapić, S. T., & Katić, V. (2016). Performance-Based Assessment Evaluated by Croatian Preschool Teachers and Students: Implications for Study Program and Practice Modifications. In D. Polly (Ed.), *Evaluating Teacher Education Programs through Performance-Based Assessments* (pp. 337–375). Hershey, PA: IGI Global. doi:10.4018/978-1-4666-9929-8.ch021

Weisberg, D. J. (2016). Methods and Strategies in Using Digital Literacy in Media and the Arts. In M. Yildiz & J. Keengwe (Eds.), *Handbook of Research on Media Literacy in the Digital Age* (pp. 456–471). Hershey, PA: IGI Global. doi:10.4018/978-1-4666-9667-9.ch022

White, E. (2017). Teacher Self-Assessment of Feedback Practices in an EFL Academic Writing Class - A Reflective Case Study. In E. Cano & G. Ion (Eds.), *Innovative Practices for Higher Education Assessment and Measurement* (pp. 162–187). Hershey, PA: IGI Global. doi:10.4018/978-1-5225-0531-0.ch009

Wyeld, T. G. (2015). Re-Visualising Giotto's 14th-Century Assisi Fresco "Exorcism of the Demons at Arezzo". In A. Ursyn (Ed.), *Handbook of Research on Maximizing Cognitive Learning through Knowledge Visualization* (pp. 358–380). Hershey, PA: IGI Global. doi:10.4018/978-1-4666-8142-2.ch012

Xu, L., Diket, R., & Brewer, T. (2015). Bringing the Arts as Data to Visualize How Knowledge Works. In A. Ursyn (Ed.), *Handbook of Research on Maximizing Cognitive Learning through Knowledge Visualization* (pp. 515–534). Hershey, PA: IGI Global. doi:10.4018/978-1-4666-8142-2.ch019

Yeh, E., Jaiswal-Oliver, M., & Posejpal, G. (2017). Global Education Professional Development: A Model for Cross-Cultural Competence. In J. Keengwe (Ed.), *Handbook of Research on Promoting Cross-Cultural Competence and Social Justice in Teacher Education* (pp. 32–51). Hershey, PA: IGI Global. doi:10.4018/978-1-5225-0897-7.ch002

Yousaf, A., Singh, M., & Gupta, A. (2017). Exploring Inter-Linkages between Cultural Intelligence and Student Satisfaction. In R. Cintron, J. Samuel, & J. Hinson (Eds.), *Accelerated Opportunity Education Models and Practices* (pp. 122–141). Hershey, PA: IGI Global. doi:10.4018/978-1-5225-0528-0.ch006

Zhou, J. (2015). Connecting the Dots: Art, Culture, Science, and Technology. In A. Ursyn (Ed.), *Handbook of Research on Maximizing Cognitive Learning through Knowledge Visualization* (pp. 345–357). Hershey, PA: IGI Global. doi:10.4018/978-1-4666-8142-2.ch011

# About the Authors

**Lisa A. Keller** earned her BS in mathematics from St. Michael's College in 1993, and her MS in mathematics from the University of Massachusetts Amherst in 2001. She received her doctorate from the University of Massachusetts Amherst in Psychometric Methods in 2002. She has fifteen years experience in the field of psychometrics. Her research interests have focused primarily on item response theory equating and scaling, reliability, and measuring student growth. She has published several articles and presented her research at national and international conferences. Dr. Keller is a member of the National Council of Measurement in Education, American Educational Research Association, the American Statistical Association and the Psychometric Society. In addition to her psychometric experience, Dr. Keller has taught mathematics to grades 7-12.

**Robert Keller** has spent ten years as an operational psychometrician in K-12 education. His primary duties in that role included performing most of the test scaling and equating for large-scale state-wide assessments for purposes of No Child Left Behind accountability systems. In addition to this, Dr. Keller was the product owner of the computer adaptive testing engine being developed for the next generation test delivery system that was simultaneously under development, as well as systems to automate, streamline, and manage data for analyzing large scale testing programs. In addition to these tasks, he has been actively engaged in research, published in peer reviewed journals, presented at national conferences, and in support of high stakes testing contracts, in the areas of scaling, equating, computer adaptive testing, and growth modeling. Dr. Keller is a member of the National Council of Measurement in Education, American Educational Research Association, and the Psychometric Society. He serves as a peer reviewer for several journals including the Journal of Educational Measurement, Applied Psychological Measurement, and the International Journal of Testing.

**Michael Nering** has over 20 years of professional psychometric experience. His research interests include person fit, item response theory, computer-based testing, and equating. He has presented and published numerous articles on a wide range of psychometric topics, and he is actively involved in the research community in various capacities. Dr. Nering is a member of the National Council of Measurement in Education, American Educational Research Association, American Psychological Association, and the Psychometric Society. For the AERA 2005 conference he was a program chair for Division D – Measurement and Research Methodology. He has also served as treasurer of the Psychometric Society, and hosted the 2008 International Meeting of the Psychometric Society. In addition, Dr. Nering has served as reviewer for several peer journals, including the Journal of Educational Measurement, Applied Psychological Measurement, Psychometrika, and the Journal of Experimental Education. In 2013 Dr. Nering was co-editor to the International Journal of Testing sponsored by the International Test Commission.

# Index

Stay Current on the Latest Emerging Research Developments

# Become an IGI Global Reviewer for Authored Book Projects

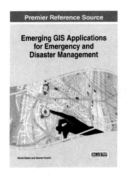   

**The overall success of an authored book project is dependent on quality and timely reviews.**

In this competitive age of scholarly publishing, constructive and timely feedback significantly decreases the turnaround time of manuscripts from submission to acceptance, allowing the publication and discovery of progressive research at a much more expeditious rate. Several IGI Global authored book projects are currently seeking highly qualified experts in the field to fill vacancies on their respective editorial review boards:

## Applications may be sent to:
development@igi-global.com

Applicants must have a doctorate (or an equivalent degree) as well as publishing and reviewing experience. Reviewers are asked to write reviews in a timely, collegial, and constructive manner. All reviewers will begin their role on an ad-hoc basis for a period of one year, and upon successful completion of this term can be considered for full editorial review board status, with the potential for a subsequent promotion to Associate Editor.

If you have a colleague that may be interested in this opportunity,
we encourage you to share this information with them.

# Become an IRMA Member

Members of the **Information Resources Management Association (IRMA)** understand the importance of community within their field of study. The Information Resources Management Association is an ideal venue through which professionals, students, and academicians can convene and share the latest industry innovations and scholarly research that is changing the field of information science and technology. Become a member today and enjoy the benefits of membership as well as the opportunity to collaborate and network with fellow experts in the field.

## IRMA Membership Benefits:

- **One FREE Journal Subscription**
- **30% Off Additional Journal Subscriptions**
- **20% Off Book Purchases**
- Updates on the latest events and research on Information Resources Management through the IRMA-L listserv.
- Updates on new open access and downloadable content added to Research IRM.
- A copy of the Information Technology Management Newsletter twice a year.
- A certificate of membership.

## IRMA Membership $195

Scan code or visit **irma-international.org** and begin by selecting your free journal subscription.

Membership is good for one full year.

Printed in the United States
By Bookmasters